FURNACE OF AFFLICTION

BY

CHRISTINE HUHS

ISBN 0-7414-3962-X

Published by:

INFINITY PUBLISHING.COM

1094 New DeHaven Street, Suite 100
West Conshohocken, PA 19428-2713
Info@buybooksontheweb.com
www.buybooksontheweb.com
Toll-free (877) BUY BOOK
Local Phone (610) 941-9999
Fax (610) 941-9959

Printed in the United States of America

Printed on Recycled Paper

Published April 2007

ACKNOWLEDGMENTS

To Jesus, my Lord and Savior! You are the author and finisher of my faith. Without you I can do nothing. You are my strength and my salvation. I love you with my whole heart. You are and always will be my "Blessed Hope".

To David; who went home to be with the Lord. He was a good and faithful servant. He revealed my Heavenly Father to me through his love and compassion. I thank God for him.

To my husband Kevin; you have stood by me through some pretty rough storms. Your love, patience, and tolerance have been greatly appreciated. I pray that God bless you richly in all things.

My sister Rose; I love you! I thank God for you!

To Daniel, my firstborn son, I hope you learn that being a parent doesn't mean that we are perfect, but that we make mistakes that can be forgiven. I pray that God bless you abundantly. I love you!

To Rachel, you understand the love a mother has for her child. I will never forget your compassion at one of the most difficult times of my life. May God's hand always rest upon you, may his peace and joy flood your soul!

DEDICATION

This story is dedicated to my youngest son Marcus. God blessed me with you and trusted me to always be there for you. It is an honor and a privilege to be your mother. If the Lord should tarry, it will bring me great pleasure to see what he has in store for your life. May God's grace and mercy be with you all the days of your life!

TABLE OF CONTENTS

INTRODUCTION

Writing this story has been the most difficult project I ever put my hand to. I pray that God will be glorified! My story is one of faith, hope and the love a mother has for her son. I've often prayed and asked God, "Why am I here? What is the purpose of my being?" I've come to know that regardless of what I think, I see the hand of God on my life from day one.

My hope is that as you read this book you will come to the knowledge that we have a heavenly father who loves us more than we can comprehend. I could have never endured the things that I have been confronted with, without my relationship with Jesus. Many times I turned my back on him and went my own way; but he was still there. God never gave up on me, and I owe it to my son to never give up on him.

Bringing up a head injury child is not an easy task. I look at Marcus and wonder what he would have been like as a normal child, without his trach. Marcus is different. He is strong, and has qualities that I only wish I could possess. For a child who has had everything taken from him, he thrives on giving. He has a heart of gold and loves life.

Putting our life on paper was very therapeutic for me. I laughed and cried remembering things that I wanted to forget. I hope you enjoy my story!

5 DAYS TO ETERNITY

"Dear God, Why are you doing this to me?" This is one of my most famous sayings. But at this particular moment on September 11, 1986, my three-year-old son Marcus was lying in the intensive care unit at a local hospital, comatose. One of my many fears had come to pass.

I'll never forget that day, a warm Thursday afternoon when the call came that one of my children was in an accident. I was at work that afternoon around four o'clock pm. The receptionist at the salon I worked for approached me, "Christine, can I talk to you in the break room?" she asked. "Sure," I responded following her to the back of the salon. "One of your children has been in an accident. They need you at the hospital," Dena said, looking as though she was about to cry. I panicked, "Which one of my boys? How was he hurt Dena?" She shook her head, "I don't know, but I'll drive you there." We hurried to Dena's car, I couldn't think straight. My heart was racing and I felt sick to my stomach. Dena didn't say much until we pulled into the emergency room parking lot. She pulled up to the door to drop me off. I'll never forget how her voice trembled as she said, "Marcus was hit by a car Christine, I'm so sorry."

Oh my God, it was my baby. Fear and anxiety swept over me as I burst through the double doors to the emergency room. To my right there was a small waiting room where I saw Marc's dad, Jimmie, standing in the doorway with a friend of his. Straight ahead were more double doors. A police officer stepped in front of me to keep me from entering. I ran past them as the officer grabbed my arm. "You can't go in there." He said. The doors opened revealing an ambulance attendant standing by a stretcher. I saw my baby lying there motionless. Everything was a blur at that moment.

I felt like I was going to pass out. My heart was racing. It was difficult to breathe. There with a nurse holding what seemed to be some sort of mask over Marc's face. Her other hand was squeezing a bag. I could tell she was pumping air into his little body. I wanted to die right there.

The officer led me out to the waiting room. Jimmie stood up as I approached him. I started screaming at him, "I hate you, look what you've done!" I was like a mad woman, beating on his face and chest. The pain I felt was excruciating. I could hardly control my crying as I made my way over to a chair to sit down. Jimmie and the officer proceeded to tell me about the accident. Marc was spending the afternoon with his father while I was at work. The officer then told me, "Marcus was playing with some other children in a residential area. He ran out in front of a car." I looked at Jimmie and asked, "Where were you?" He said, "I was in the house, getting ready to go." He responded. "I stopped by to see an old friend of mine, Nathan. I let Marc play outside with the kids." I couldn't believe this was happening. "An older lady was driving the car that hit your son; she is very upset so they took her to the hospital." The officer told us. My heart went out to this woman. "They are transferring Marcus to a nearby hospital that has a pediatric intensive care unit." He added. Jimmie and I sat in that waiting room, what seemed like a lifetime.

A doctor finally came to tell us they had taken Marc to the other hospital. Jimmie and I got into his car and drove over there. Once inside, we were instructed to go to the fifth floor where they had taken Marc. I couldn't wait to see him. It was about five o'clock pm. I had to call home. Daniel would be wondering where we were by now. He was my ten year old. I knew he would be home from school. I got Dan on the phone and told him that Marc was in the hospital. Jimmie would be there to pick him up after we talked to the doctors.

I tried to get into the room where they had Marc but the nurses wouldn't let me in. I looked through the window to see several nurses cleaning up Marc wounds. I could see where he was hit on the right side of his face. They were hooking him up to all kinds of gadgets. He looked so tiny and innocent lying there. I could tell he was fighting for his life. I kept asking the nurses as they walked by, "How is he? Is he going to be ok?" They'd just tell me, "A doctor will be with you soon." I hated the waiting. The hospital staff put Jimmie and me in a waiting room across the hall. It had a couple of chairs, a twin bed and a television in it. The nurse told us that they called our pediatrician, Dr. Henry, and a neurosurgeon. They would be in to see us as soon as they got done with Marc's exam.

Our doctors finally came to see us. Jimmie and I anxiously wanted to hear the diagnosis. "Your son has a twisted brain stem. It's severe; it almost always takes their life. I'm sorry but there is nothing we can do but wait." I wanted to die. I ran into the bathroom, pleading with God! "Please don't take him, I can't handle this." I cried. My insides hurt from the pain I was feeling. "Please, take me; don't leave me here without him. Why are you doing this? What have I done to deserve my son dying?"

I came out of the bathroom sick to my stomach. Jimmie was sitting in a chair with his head down in his hands. As I walked towards the sofa, he looked up at me and said "We can go in to see Marc in a few minutes." Jimmie and I sat there in silence. I didn't want to hear anything he had to say and he knew it. I was furious with him. I remembered thinking, "How are we ever going to get through this?"

A nurse finally came to get us. The moment I laid eyes on my baby laying on that bed the tears began again. I could feel his pain. The right side of his face had a few stitches. It was so swollen I couldn't see his right eye.

I couldn't reach him to kiss his face; there were tubes and wires running everywhere. I could only reach his feet. At that moment Jimmie said, "I'll go get Daniel and a few things we will need while we are here." I was angry with this man but I was glad he was with me. I had no one to call. I was scared. The staff allowed us to stay in the room with Marc. They had a recliner beside his bed. Jimmie returned with Dan a short while later and we set up camp in the room across the hall. That first night was the longest night of my life. We hadn't eaten or slept. Jimmie and I stayed close to Marcus all night and talked. He finally gave me some details of the accident. "I heard tires screeching and the kids screaming," he told me. "I ran out to see Marcus' body laying up the street on a curb." I tried to envision this as Jimmie was describing it. He went on to say, "The police and ambulance arrived in a matter of minutes. They didn't think Marcus was alive!" I could tell Jimmie was having a hard time with this.

We made it through the night; Marcus was still with us. Jimmie got Daniel to school that morning. We sat by Marcus' side most of the day. A woman came to see me later that afternoon from Social Services. She had a lot of papers for me to fill out. I told her we had no insurance and she immediately applied for a state medical card for us. I was so grateful to her. She also gave me vouchers for the hospital cafeteria so we would be able to feed Dan. That evening Jimmie and I were standing outside Marcus' room talking. I saw a man coming down the hallway towards us. He looked peculiar, an older man wearing a long black trench coat and a black hat. He removed his hat as he approached Jimmie walking down the hall to meet him. His gray hair and glasses gave him a distinguished appearance. They stood there for a couple minutes talking. I wondered who this strange man was. I knew I had never seen him before.

The two of them started walking towards me as I looked in this man's face. He looked rugged. "Christine, this is David, he was at the scene of Marc's accident." I extended my hand and looked in his eyes as I said, "it's nice to meet you David." I had no idea at that moment how much my life was about to change.

There was something about this man; but I couldn't figure out what it was. "David would like to pray with Marcus, is that ok?" Jimmie said as he interrupted my thoughts. "Sure, if you think it will help," was my response. My attitude towards God was at an all time low. All I knew was that I was being punished for something. David followed Jimmie and me into the intensive care unit. David said, "I saw him get hit by the car." Why didn't Jimmie tell me about this man? I'd find out as soon as David left. Jimmie told the nurse that we were going to pray so she stepped out of the room. David walked over to Marc's bedside. I saw him lay his hand on Marc's stomach and began to pray. I never heard anything like this in my life. It was the most wonderful prayer I ever heard. The room filled with such a sweet, calm presence as he thanked God for Marcus' recovery. He thanked God for healing Marcus from the top of his head to the soles of his feet. He asked God for healing, then began to thank him that it was already done. I didn't know what to think. I followed Jimmie and David to our room across the hall. We all sat down and David said, "I would like to pray for the two of you as well." He reassured me, "God is healing your baby, and he doesn't want to take him from you." I couldn't help thinking that this man was not real. David also told me, "You should continually thank God for Marcus' life."

Jimmie and I were in a daze. David began to pray for us in that little room. It's amazing when we have nothing to hold on to, how desperately we will grasp whatever is within our reach. David left us that day as quickly as he appeared.

He left me with plenty to think about. I didn't know God. What I did know of him scared me to death. Now I was being told to depend on him because he was the only one who was able to save Marcus' life. I was still hurting so much inside. I was truly convinced that my life was over. I didn't want to depend on God. My life up to this point had been a living hell. God had not been there before, or at least, not that I knew of. But I was very curious about this David. Jimmie told me that David was the one who called the ambulance that day; that he prayed over Marcus at the scene of the accident. That was all I knew about this man.

It was day three at the hospital. Marcus was still with us. We never left him. One of us was always there with him. Jimmie was getting Daniel to and from school. Dan wasn't very happy about our temporary living arrangements but we made do. Jimmie and I still hadn't slept or hardly eaten. We felt so helpless. I would sit beside Marcs' bed rubbing his feet, talking to him. I would see tears roll down his cheeks; the nurses would tell me to keep talking. They believed that he could hear us; that he knew we were there. He was so precious, a wonderful, healthy, happy three year old that brought us so much joy. Dr. Henry came in everyday to see Marcus. "He is stable, but still in critical condition, we will just have to wait and see what happens" are the words we heard after three days. Jimmie and I were exhausted. This was taking a toll on all of us. My boss from the salon came to see me the next day. "I can't come back to work right now," I told her. "My baby is in a coma! I have to be here with him". I knew she felt bad saying it, "I'll have to let you go, I need to fill your position," she said. I was upset; but I really didn't care. I knew if Marcus didn't make it I was going to die also. This was selfish of me; I had another child to take care of. I didn't think I could handle the pain of losing my baby. I was blaming Jimmie for not watching him but when you get right down to it, I felt as though I were the guilty one.

What had I done in my lifetime to cause this horrible thing to happen to my child? He was innocent and undeserving of this. David came back to see us again. We talked for a few minutes then went into Marc's room to pray again. I couldn't help notice how this man prayed for Marcus. This time he never asked God to heal him; he just kept thanking him for it. David wanted to pray for us again, so we went across the hall. As this man started praying for us I wept. I didn't want him to stop. There was such heaviness in the room that I couldn't move. I never felt so relaxed and peaceful. When David stood up to leave he pulled out his wallet. "Jesus put this in here for you today," he said as he handed us a twenty-dollar bill. We were so broke. I was really drawn to this man. "Where did he come from?" I thought. He didn't know us; we surely didn't know him.

It's now been five days since the accident. Marcus was still in the coma. I could see the battle going on inside of him. "It looks like Marcus is going to make it!" Dr. Henry said during his morning visit. "There is a good chance that he may be blind, deaf, or even in a state of vegetation." Those words kept ringing in my ears. I cried, "My baby is not going to die!" Jimmie and I just hugged each other crying tears of relieve. We couldn't wait to see David again. We found ourselves looking for him. Sure enough, that evening he stopped in to see us. We told him the news. David once again laid hands on Marcus and prayed, "Father, I thank you for healing this boy! I thank you that there is no crippling, no deafness or blindness, and I thank you in Jesus' name." This time I believed what David was praying. Later that evening David and I walked down to another waiting area on the fifth floor of that hospital. David gave me an invitation to meet the real Jesus. I took him up on that invitation that night. The Jesus that I had heard about as a child was now a reality to me in just five days.

THE BEGINNING

I have a lot of childhood memories growing up in a small town in Northwestern Pennsylvania. Some of them are good, but most of them not so good. I was born into a family that already had nine grown children. My mother had been divorced for a while when she met my father. It wasn't long before she found out she was pregnant with me. My brothers and sisters were having families of their own. Joe was the youngest of my mom's other nine children. He was about six years old when I was born, so I grew up with him. I don't remember much about the first few years of my life but I knew that I didn't see much of my parents. My mom and dad both worked for a chair factory. It wasn't until I was about school age that I realized that my parents spent most of their time at a local bar; that is where their money went. We never lived in the same house for more than six months. They would get evicted and have to stay for a while at a local hotel. I would end up staying with one of my sisters. I hated living with them. As Joe and I got older he started taking care of me.

Joe was good about making sure I got in at night. He would get me up in the mornings for school because mom and dad went to work very early. I loved Joe. I grew dependant upon him for my care. We were living in a small trailer behind my Aunt Wilma's house (my mom's sister), when mom came home one Saturday afternoon, "Your dad is moving out." She told me. I was nearly eight years old at the time. I felt sorry for my dad. I was his only child. My father moved into a one-room apartment. It was located above the bar he and my mom went to everyday after work. To me, my father was a functioning alcoholic. He drank so much but never missed work. I would laugh and say, "If dad and mom missed work they wouldn't have any money to drink on."

I loved my grandparents; (my mothers' parents), though I didn't see them much. They lived a lifestyle different than ours that included them attending church all the time. They didn't approve of the way my mom lived. My Aunt Mae, mom's sister went to the same church as my grandparents. Her daughter Janet was my best friend growing up. Mom called them "Holy Rollers." I often wondered what she meant by that. I would go to church with them once in a while. I really enjoyed it! They would sing, clap their hands and get excited. But my grandmother would cry a lot. I didn't understand why. My Aunt didn't like Janet at my house. We had a television and my aunt said it was a sin to watch or even own one. I would laugh and tell Janet, "You're going to hell if you don't get away from the TV." She would just sit there in front of it until someone pulled her away. As you can probably tell, Janet was my only friend beside Joe. Parents of the kids I went to school with called my dad a "town drunk." Because of this, I had a hard time making friends.

Joe graduated from high school in 1968. We were all so proud of him. He got a job and bought himself a car. He went to Chicago that summer to visit one of his friends. I'll never forget how much I missed him. In the fall, his friends were all enlisting in different branches of the military. He took all of the tests to enlist with his friends but couldn't pass them because of his eyesight. His friends all left; he stayed home and worked. I turned thirteen in May of 1969. School had just got out that first week of June. I remember walking in the front door to be met by mom. She was upset and crying as she said, "Grandpa is in the hospital, he had a heart attack." My grandpa was eighty-one years old. "We need to go stay with grandma," mom added, "Grandpa is not doing well." I really did not to want to go but I did. It was Friday, June 13, 1969; we were still at grandmas'.

Joe stopped in for some dinner with us that evening. "Larry and John are home on leave from the Navy this weekend," Joe told mom. He added with a grin, "We are going out tonight." Mom just looked at him, "Where are you going?" she asked. "We are going to New York State," he told her. I knew what they did up there. New York State line was about fifteen miles from where we lived. All of the high school students went up there on weekends to drink. They had a legal drinking age of eighteen back then. Unfortunately, some of the students never made it back. I remember sitting there thinking how happy Joe looked. He had such a rotten childhood. Things were looking up for him. I loved him dearly. Mom interrupted my thoughts, "You better be careful, it's raining tonight," she told him. "Mom, don't worry, nothing is going to happen to me," he told her as he went out the door.

It was a rainy night that night; I remember it well. I went to sleep in the bedroom right off the kitchen. I woke up at what seemed to be the middle of the night to a lot of commotion in the kitchen. I heard my grandmother crying hysterically and Martha, (one of my sisters') say, "The police have mom out on the porch; Joe was killed tonight in a car accident." I heard those words echo in my mind over and over again, "Joe was killed." Then it hit me; Joe wasn't coming back. I was never going to see him again. "Oh God, not my Joe," I said as tears began to burn my eyes. I was thirteen years old. The only person that cared about me was gone forever. I crawled back in the bed and cried myself to sleep. The next couple of days for me were a nightmare. I didn't talk and I couldn't cry. My mom and grandmother were grieving; I didn't know how to grieve. I was angry! God took my brother and I didn't know why. On Monday morning, two days after Joe's accident, my mom woke me and tearfully said, "Your grandfather passed away this morning."

We now had two funerals to prepare for. My mom was a mess, losing her father and son in a matter of days. I felt my heart grow cold towards her. Why did God have to take Joe, I needed him. I didn't know my mother. We never had any kind of relationship. Joe was gone! I had to deal with it. I never thought that those words he spoke to mom that night, "Don't worry, nothing is going to happen to me," would be the last time I'd hear his voice. The smile he had on his face as he ran out the door would stay with me for the rest of my life.

I started junior high school in the fall of 1969. I hated it because Aunt Mae sent Janet away to a Christian School in West Virginia. She was my only real friend and I was going to miss her. "I hate going to Christian School, I don't want to go," she would tell me. "You must be crazy, I'd give anything to be in your shoes," I'd tell her. I envied her so much! She lived in the same house all her life, with the same parents who loved her. They provided for her. In my eyes, going away to private school was the ultimate. Janet was getting ready to go and wouldn't be back till Christmas break.

My first year in high school wasn't so bad. I made a couple of friends but for the most part I was avoided. I didn't care; my mom quit drinking when Joe died. We lived in the same house for almost a year by the time school was out. We didn't have a relationship, but I had a roof over my head, and food to eat, so I was content. My life wasn't much fun though, I grew up very fast. I didn't get too close to anyone for fear of losing them.

I was fifteen years old when boys got my attention. I met these three boys at my neighbors' house one afternoon. They lived in Wattsburg. It was a small town about eight miles from Union City, my hometown. They were brothers, and I really liked Brian.

He was the oldest of the three boys. Brian and I couldn't see one another very often because he went to a different school.

His mother would bring him to Union City once in a while. We spent a lot of time on the phone. He told me how his father was an alcoholic and was killed in an accident just before we met. I told him about my life and Joe's death. I finally had someone to talk to. It was great! Brian and I got close but his mother wasn't happy about it. I knew she didn't like me. I was sixteen when mom told me, "we are moving to Erie." I didn't want to move to Erie! "Mom," I screamed at her, "I don't want to go; I don't want to change schools." She explained, "I'm going to get a job up there. I found us a place to live." That was that. It was also a big mistake. I already knew how to live in the streets and a city was one place I didn't need to be. I hated the school so I dropped out. Brian graduated from high school and enlisted in the Army. He had to go away to boot camp. "As soon as I get out of the basic training I will come home and we will get married." He told me. I was so excited! I could hardly wait.

Here I was living in the city with my mom. It was the summer of 1973. What a great summer it was! Janet came home from school. We had big plans. We started hanging out at all the wrong places, with all the wrong people. It wasn't long before we were introduced to marijuana. We were smoking it all the time. We went to parties and met lots of people. Brian was in New Jersey for his basic training. I was in Erie having a blast! Janet was so rebellious; I knew she wasn't going back to school in the fall. She would fight with my Aunt Mae and I would get upset with her. She had a good mom but she didn't appreciate her. I loved Janet! We were best friends. "Don't get married," she would tell me. "I don't want you to go." Brian told me that we were moving to Kansas after we got married.

"You don't know what it is like for me living here Janet," I'd say. "I have no one but Brian to take care of me, I have to go." I told her, "Mom told me as soon as I got married and moved away, she was going to Florida to live with my oldest brother Jack." I knew my mom wanted me to go as badly as I wanted to.

Brian came home a couple of weeks before our wedding in October of 1973. I was now seventeen. I couldn't wait to move to Kansas. "Brian, you want to get high?" I said as we were going down the highway towards the city one night. He gave me the weirdest look as I pulled it out of my bag. "Where did you get that?" he asked me. "From Ron and Diane," I said with a grin. They were a married couple I had met over the summer. That night Brian and I chose the path we were going to take. It wasn't a good one but we didn't care. We were married a couple weeks later and left on our journey to Ft. Riley, Kansas.

I'll never forget the day we pulled into Manhattan, a small college town right outside of Ft. Riley. It was a warm autumn day. The sun was shining; it was beautiful. The town was so clean with a lot of older but well kept buildings. We stopped for a newspaper to start our hunt for our first apartment together. We found an adorable one-bedroom apartment with a fireplace in a four-plex apartment building. The neighborhood was older with charming houses and huge trees that lined the street. I was in heaven. I was in my own home, away from my mother. It felt so good! My mother never abused me or anything like that, I think my resentment towards her stemmed from her not caring for me, or trying to know me. I was her daughter! I needed a relationship with her, which she denied me.

It took about a week for me to hate military life. Brian came home from work one night and said, "I have to pull guard duty tomorrow night."

"What's that?" I responded. "I have to stand a post all night on the base." Then he decided to break the other bad news to me, "Next month I will be in the field for a week, playing war games," as he called them. I hated to be alone; I was afraid. I knew I would have to get used to it, we were in this for four years. Time went by fast. In the spring we decided to move to Ogden. It was a very small military town closer to the fort. We moved into a trailer park. I loved it, everyone that lived there were just like us. We were young, in the military, and away from home. Some had children and some didn't. I made friends fast in that little town.

There was a black family that lived across the street from us. I decided to go over to meet them. Lynn was a small petite woman, about my age. Her husband Jimmie was in the Army also. They were from Louisiana. Lynn and Jimmie had 2 small boys. We spent a lot of time together. It wasn't long before we all became good friends.

I was a horrible wife to Brian. I didn't know how to be a wife. We would fight all the time. "I'm being transferred to Germany in January," Brian told me one night as we were having dinner. "I can't take you with me." I was furious, "They can't do that," I said as fear swept over me. "It's only for sixteen months," he said as he was trying to calm me down. I loved Brian. Now the Army was taking him away from me. This was December 1975. He had to report to Germany the middle of February 1976. "I'm taking you home, you can't stay here," he said. "Oh God, no, I don't want to go home," I told him. Brian was firm on his decision to take me home. My mom had moved back to Erie. She was living with one of my sisters, Martha. She was going through a divorce and had two children that needed someone to watch them while she worked. Mom moved back to help her. Martha and I never got along very well.

"You can stay with your mom and sister, or I'm sure you could stay with my mom," Brian said. I just looked at him with disgust. The hell I got away from, I now had to go back to.

Brian and I arrived in Erie the end of January. It was cold. Erie had so much snow. I didn't miss the Pennsylvania winters while we were in Kansas. It got cold but it didn't snow as much. Brian left me at my sisters' house with my mom. He wanted to go home to his mothers', and I didn't want to go. He picked me up the next day so we could talk about what we were going to do. "I know you don't want to be here," Brian said. "As soon as I get paid, I will start sending you money. You can find a place to live." I agreed. About a week later Brian left for Germany. I was very afraid of what was going to happen to us. Would we survive this separation? In my heart I knew we wouldn't.

It wasn't long after Brian left that Martha and I were at one another's throat. I couldn't do anything right. "When your husband sends you money, I want it. You're going to pay me for staying here," Martha said. "I have to find my own place to live with the money he sends me," I told her. We argued back and forth for a while. Later Mom told me, "Don't fight with her, you know how she is." "I know," I said, "I hate her! I don't want to be here." A few days later mom handed me an envelope. It was a letter from Brian! There was a money order tucked inside for one hundred dollars! "You better cash that so you can give some of it to your sister," mom said. "I'm not giving her anything," I snapped. "I'm going to save this." Mom just glared at me. "When the next money order comes, I will have enough to get out of here," I told her. I ran out of the house slamming the door behind me. I was going to cash the money order and go to the store. I needed a few things. I had about eighty dollars left so I hid it in my wallet. I got back home around dinnertime; it was dark and snowing again. I hated the snow.

I tried to open the door; it was locked. I knocked on the door a few times. "Do you have money for me?" Martha asked as she cracked the door open. "No, I don't!" I replied. All I could hear, as she was slamming the door in my face was, "You're not staying here, get off my porch." I started to cry,

"Can I have my clothes," I pleaded. Martha wouldn't open the door, so I left. I started walking down the street. Oh God, what was I going to do? I had eighty dollars in my pocket with nowhere to go. It was now snowing so hard I could barely see in front of me. Tears were stinging my face. I went to a pay phone to call my sisters' house. Mom answered. "Mom, can you get my clothes for me?" I asked. "I can come by tomorrow and pick them up." I could hear Martha in the background; "She can have her clothes when she gives me the one hundred dollars she got from Brian." Mom yelled, "Give her the money so you can stop this fighting." I told mom, "I only have eighty dollars left. I'm not giving it to her!" I slammed the phone down and started walking.

I didn't know where I was going or what I was going to do. I thought about calling Brian's mom, but she was 15 miles away. I knew she wasn't going to come out in this snowstorm to get me. It was getting late. I had to find a place to keep the wind off me. I ducked into the entryway of a building and squatted down to keep myself warm. I cried so hard, "Why was this happening to me?" About an hour had gone by; I was freezing to say the least. I looked out towards the street. There wasn't much traffic that night. I saw some light from a streetlight. I could see that the snow was letting up. "Are you all right there honey?" I heard an older woman say. I could see her standing in the entryway. "I'm ok," I replied. "I got into a fight with my sister tonight; she made me leave." I paused. "I don't have anywhere to go."

She extended her hand for mine and said "I'm Anna; let me help you to your feet." I got to my feet, not sure of what was going to happen next. "I work at the boarding house down the street, I was just on my way in when I heard crying over here." She smiled and said, "Come on, let us put you up for the night." Someone was sure looking out for me that night. I went with Anna. I found out she was a nun. She took me inside this building, then up a flight of stairs. We went into a room that had four twin beds in it. I looked on the other side of the room. There was a young woman talking to a little girl. She was telling the little girl, "Go to sleep; everything is going to be all right." Anna handed me a flannel nightgown and said, "This will keep you warm tonight." Then she pulled down the covers on a small twin bed in the corner of the room. "Sleep good," she said as she left the room. I went into the bathroom to get out of my wet clothes. The nightgown smelled so good; it felt so warm on my freezing body. I crawled in the bed pulling the covers over my head. I thanked God for taking care of me that night.

The next morning I couldn't wait to get out of there. I got dressed and thanked them for the room. I had to get to a pay phone to call mom. I knew Martha would be at work. I wanted to get my things. When mom answered the phone I asked, "Can I come by to get my things?" Mom told me, "Martha has them all locked up in the trunk of her car." Mom went on to say, "She is not going to give them to you until you pay her." I couldn't believe this was happening. "I get paid in a few days, I guess I can pay her for you," mom said with hesitation. "Ok mom, I'll call back in a few days," I told her as I was fighting back tears. I wasn't angry anymore; I was hurt. I got off the phone and went to get a newspaper. I had all day to find me a place to stay. I started looking in the "rooms for rent" section. Before long I found one. It was in a decent neighborhood. It cost me forty dollars a week. I was so happy!

I went to a thrift store to buy a couple pans, a few dishes, a pillow and a blanket. Then I went to the grocery store and bought a few things I could survive on. I sat in that little room for a few days trying to decide what I was going to do with my life. I knew this was a temporary situation. I was going back to Kansas but I wasn't sure how I was going to get there. I called mom back and she let me come get my things. When I arrived at my sister's house, mom met me outside. "I'm going back to Kansas," I told her. "I can't stay here." She looked at me and asked, "How are you going to get there?" I didn't know at the time, but I told her, "I will get the money for a bus." Mom stood there looking at me, not saying a word. I stepped down off the porch to walk away when I heard the screen door close behind her as she went back inside the house. Tears started burning my eyes but I refused to cry. I held back those tears convincing myself that I didn't need her.

I headed down the main street of the city carrying my bags. I walked right by a friend of Brian's. He turned to look back at me and said, "Hey, aren't you Brian's wife?" I said, "Yes, I am." I looked at him remembering who he was. "Dave Miller, right?" I asked. "Yes, where is Brian?" he asked me. We started walking as I told him that Brian was in Germany. "Let me help you with these bags," he offered, taking two of them. My room was a few blocks away so he walked me home. When we arrived at my room, I offered him to stay a while. I made us a couple of sandwiches. "What have you been doing since high school?" I asked him. I couldn't believe what he was telling me, "I've been traveling all over the states, I went to California; I'm going to Florida soon," he said. The next thing I knew he was telling me, "I hitchhike everywhere I go." I was amazed! The thought immediately entered my mind, hitchhiking to Kansas! Before I knew it the words were coming out of my mouth, "Do you think you could get me to Kansas?"

He looked at me bewildered and said, "You don't want to do that!" I said, "Oh yes I do, more than anything." We talked about it for hours. The next thing I knew, we were leaving the next morning. He left later that night telling me, "I will be over to pick you up in the morning." I was so anxious I could hardly sleep. I kept thinking, "He won't show up." I had to get out of here! I didn't know any other way to do it.

It was a long night but Dave showed up at my door at the crack of dawn. I was so happy to see him. I left that little room with the pans and dishes still there. Dave and I started our walk to Kansas. I had seven dollars in my pocket. I had no idea of what I was going to do once I got there. I had a lot of pain and unforgiveness deep down inside me. I just wanted to forget everything. I was about to enter into another phase of my life. One thing I knew, I was a survivor. I'd been doing it all my life. I knew Dave and I would make it to Kansas because I knew in my heart that was where I was supposed to be. This was going to be a new beginning for me. I didn't know where I was going to stay but had a good idea. I was going to start with Jimmie and Lynn back at our old trailer park in Ogden.

ANXIETY

Jimmie was surprised to see Dave and me standing at his door this one Sunday afternoon in February of 1976. It was so cold out; a mix of rain and snow were hitting my face. "Hi, can we come in?" I said, hoping that he wouldn't turn us away. "Sure, come on it, its pretty nasty out there today," he said as he was looking at Dave. I'm sure he was wondering, "Who is this man, where is Brian?" Reading Jimmie's thoughts I said, "Jimmie, this is Dave, a friend of ours from Pennsylvania." Dave extended his hand and said "Nice to meet you." Jimmie, Dave and I sat down in the living room of the small trailer. I proceeded to tell Jimmie how I came back to Kansas and why. "Could I please stay here with you and Lynn until I can find my own place to live?" I asked him. "Christine, I just got back from Louisiana." He added, "Lynn wanted to go home so I took her and the kids' home this weekend." He paused for a second, as I could tell he was thinking this over. "You're more than welcome to stay here for as long as you need," he finally said. I gave a sigh of relief. "This isn't going to look good." I thought. But I had nowhere else to go.

Dave stayed with us that night. The next morning he was getting ready to leave, "Dave, I don't know how to thank you for bringing me back to Kansas, I don't know what I would have done with out you. Thank you so much!" Dave just looked at me with a concerned look on his face, "You just take care of yourself," he said as he was leaving. I watched Dave start walking down the road, thanking God we made it. I was more than ready to get on with my new life.

I liked Jimmie; we spent a lot of time talking. He was still in the Army, so he went to work everyday. After being there about a week I asked him, "Could I possibly use your car tomorrow, I have some errands I need to run?" I hated asking him but I had to get some things done.

I wasn't feeling well. I needed to get to a doctor. "Sure," he told me. "You can take me to work. I'll get a ride home at the end of the day." I was so excited. Jimmie was good to me. I was falling for him; I had an attraction to him. I found myself cooking him dinner and doing his laundry. This was not good, but I was enjoying it. Apparently he was too. Wasn't too long before I heard, "I love you Christine," he said one night after dinner. We made love. That was the beginning of our relationship. I already knew in my heart that I wanted a divorce from Brian. The only thing I felt bad about was Jimmie being married, not only that, but Lynn was my friend. He reassured me, "Lynn and I are divorcing Christine, our marriage has been over for a long time." But somehow that didn't remove the guilt I was feeling.

The next morning I called the doctors office back for the results of my physical. "You're pregnant," the nurse told me. I was so excited. "A baby," I thought. This is truly an answer to prayer. I got off the phone with the nurse. It didn't take long for reality to set in. I'm living with a married black man, divorcing my husband, and I'm pregnant. "Oh Lord, what have I gotten myself into?" I thought. All day I kept thinking of how to tell Jimmie. I knew in my heart that he would be happy for me. He knew how much I wanted a baby for a long time. I had dinner prepared for Jimmie when he got home that night. "I called the doctor back today, I'm pregnant," I told him. He glared at me as I went on to say, "I want to move to Manhattan." I could tell at that moment he wasn't as happy as I thought he would be. "I guess we could move to Manhattan," he said as he got up from the table. "If the baby is a boy Christine, you need to give it to Brian." I couldn't believe what I was hearing. "A white boy needs to be raised by his white father, not a black man," he continued. "If the baby is a girl, you can keep her."

I was so hurt; I got up from the table and left the room. Jimmie and I didn't talk much the rest of the night. "What is this black and white nonsense?" I thought. I convinced myself that night that Jimmie would change his mind by the time the baby was born. I was not giving up my baby!

It was April of 1976 when Jimmie and I moved into an apartment in Manhattan. The baby was due in October and I had a lot to do. Jimmie let me use his car for my doctors' appointments and to run my errands. I was starting to look pregnant. However; I was not feeling real good about myself. I read every book I could get my hands on about pregnancy. I had morning sickness for a while; it wasn't too bad. It didn't last for more than a few months. I cried a lot. I was feeling guilty about Brian. He was excited about the baby, but I still hadn't told him I was getting a divorce. Brian was still in Germany so airmail letters were our only means of communication. He was taking a leave from the Army to come home in October when the baby was due.

I felt like I had been pregnant forever. "Brian will be home soon," I told Jimmie one Saturday morning. "The baby is due in less than a month; I don't know how to tell him I want a divorce," I added. Jimmie was getting out of the Army on October 13th that year. He was very excited about it. "I'm going to be leaving town for a couple weeks after I get out of the Army," he told me. I was relieved for that but still didn't know how to tell Brian I was getting a divorce. Brian showed up just in time. He arrived on Saturday. The baby came on Monday. I named him Daniel. What a precious baby. A few days later Brian and I took him back to my apartment. The night before Brian had to return to Germany I hit him with the divorce. "Brian, I really need to talk to you, I don't want to be married anymore. I want a divorce," I said waiting on his reaction. "Why, why now?" he said. I sat there in silence, speechless. He called a cab to take him to the airport.

Daniel was asleep in his carrier on the sofa. Brian picked up the carrier and said, “I’m taking my son with me!” I panicked! The next thing I knew we both had a hold of the carrier. I was crying, “No, no! You can’t have him, he’s mine!” Brian let go of Daniel and stormed out the door.

I thought about that night a lot over the next couple of weeks. “I just made a horrible mistake,” I told myself. I felt bad about it, but I wasn’t in love with Brian. I wasn’t good for him. “What about Daniel?” I’d think. I knew deep down he deserved to have his father but finally convinced myself I did the right thing. Jimmie got back from his vacation. I was happy to see him. “How did it go with Brian?” he asked. I told him everything that happened that night. “I’m keeping my baby, Jimmie,” I told him. I could see the disappointment in his eyes as he said, “I think it’s a mistake for us to be together Christine, I’m thinking about your son, how will this affect him?” We left it at that, and didn’t talk about it again.

It wasn’t long before my family found out I was living with Jimmie. My mother was sick about it. “How can you do this?” she asked me on the phone one day. I said, “I love him, he is good to us.” She went on to inform me, “You no longer have a family here.” I could care less. I never had a family anyway. I still kept in touch with my mother, sending her pictures of Dan as he was growing. It was June of 1977 when I got pregnant again. I had terrible morning sickness and in August I started bleeding. My doctor put me on bed rest but it didn’t help. One day in October I was cramping badly and made an appointment to see him. At the moment my doctor came into the room I was miscarrying. Once again I felt that familiar pain of death. I couldn’t believe I lost my baby. At least I still had Daniel.

About a year had gone by when I decided to tell Jimmie, “I want to go home, back to Pennsylvania.” I was surprised when he said, “Let me think about it.” I wanted to go back for Dan more than anything. He was two years old now and I wanted him to know his father's family. It was November 1978 and we made the move. Jimmie and I found an apartment in Erie. I couldn't wait to see my dad. He knew I was with Jimmie. I had not seen, nor talked to my dad in 5 years. Surely he would be glad to see me. I knew he would love his grandson. It was the first week in December, cold and snowy, when I decided to drive to Union City to see my father. He got off work everyday at 4:00, so I waited outside the chair factory for him. I saw my dad walk out of the building. I felt like a little girl again. "Dad," I yelled. I was so happy to see him. He looked over at the car. As he walked towards us I yelled, "Hi dad, I moved to Erie last month. This is Daniel, my son; he is two years old now." At that moment I realized I was rambling. I went on to say, "We would like you to come and spend Christmas Day with us." Right then I felt like a knife went into my back. He wasn't happy to see me. "I already have plans for Christmas this year," he said, "I have to go now." My father walked away from me. The tears were stinging my eyes once again. I cried all the way back to Erie that night. Dan and I walked in the door of the apartment. Jimmie was sitting on the sofa in the living room. "What happened?" he asked. "I don't want to talk about it," I replied.

A couple of months went by. It was one of the worst winters. Jimmie couldn't find a job. I was lonely. I wanted to go back to Kansas. We decided it was the best thing to do. I loved my father so much but I knew I would never see him again. We left Erie in February of 1979 headed back to Kansas. Not long after we got there I decided I needed to do something with my life.

I enrolled in a Beauty College and decided to become a cosmetologist that spring of 1979. Classes started in the fall. I was so excited. Dan was going to a preschool at the time. In May I found out I was pregnant again. Jimmie and I wanted this baby. I called my mom to tell her the news. I told her about the last baby that I had lost; that I really hoped I would carry this one. "You should not be bringing a bi-racial baby into this world, it's not right," she said. "God will punish you for this." I didn't want to hear any more she had to say about it.

Brian and I were divorced about the same time that Jimmie's divorce was final. One afternoon I got a call from my mom, "I thought you would like to know, Janet and Robin were killed last night in a car accident." She said. I was devastated. Robin was Janet's seventeen-year-old sister. Janet had a baby the year before with a guy she was living with. I still had not seen the baby. "Why God?" I thought as I hung up the phone. Why not me?" I hated life! I felt that my punishment was to live it. I really believed that God was going to take every person away from me that I loved.

Jimmie and I decided that we should get married. Since I was pregnant we planned on an October wedding. Jimmie called his mom one evening in June. He told her about the baby and the wedding. He called her "Big Mama." He got off the phone and said, "I invited mama to come for a visit." I was so anxious to meet her!

October 1st of 1979 I was six months pregnant when I started bleeding. I went to see my doctor. He ordered an ultra sound the next day to check for placenta privia. I never had an ultra sound before; it was so awesome. I could see the babies' hands and feet. I could also see that the baby was a boy! They couldn't detect any abnormalities so I went home. The doctor once again put me on bed rest. This was a Friday afternoon. Jimmie and I had a long weekend.

My mother's words echoed over and over again in my mind, "God's going to punish you for this." I kept pushing the thoughts out of my mind. I didn't have the heart to tell Jimmie what she said. Sunday night Jimmie took me to the hospital. I went into labor and delivered a little boy. He didn't make it. I was heart broken. I've lost another baby. "He looked just like you Christine," Jimmie said, trying to comfort me. The nurses took me into the operating room where my doctor did a DNC.

I woke up Monday morning seeing Jimmie sitting in a chair beside my bed. "Are you all right?" he asked. "I'm ok, I want to go home," I told him. I was hurting inside, totally confused. I kept thinking, "What was wrong with me? Was I being punished for what I did to Brian? Was God killing my babies?" I had a feeling I'd never know the answers to these questions.

The end of October came and Big Mama was coming for our wedding. After losing the baby, I really wasn't sure I wanted to marry Jimmie. We lived together all of those years. I knew we should be married but something just didn't feel right. Jimmie went to pick up Big Mama at the bus station one evening. I couldn't wait for them to get home. When they walked in the door, I took one look at her. I immediately knew she was a wonderful woman. "I'm finally meeting the woman who has kept my baby in Kansas all this time," she said with a warm smile. "Hi Big Mama," I said, as she gave me a big hug. I loved this woman. We talked for hours. She told me stories. I could tell Jimmie had a close family. I envied him for that. Jimmie and I had a nice small wedding. A few days later Big Mama had to go back home. I went back to school to do my last couple of months so I could graduate.

It was a Monday morning, following Thanksgiving weekend, about 6:00 am when our phone rang. I answered, "Hello." I heard my mothers' voice on the other end, "Your father died." There was silence. "You need to come home to take care of his funeral arrangements," She said. I told her I would be there. I woke Jimmie; "I have to get on a plane today for Erie, my dad died." I would be there for five days but I would have to bring a bus back because we couldn't afford round trip airfare. I was okay with that. I got on the plane dreading what was in store for me. I didn't want to see my mother or anyone else for that matter. My mother and one of my sisters picked me up at the airport that afternoon. Of course it was snowing like crazy. We went straight to the funeral home. I got started on the funeral arrangements. Dad had very little life insurance but I made do with what was there.

Mom and I were sitting at the kitchen table at one of my sisters' house that evening. I was so tired; it had been a long day. "I think your dad knew he was going to die," Mom said. "He took a bus to Erie last Wednesday night looking for you." I was stunned! Dad was looking for me?" I asked, not sure I heard her right. "Yes," she said, "A friend of his told me your dad wanted to make things right with you." I started to cry, for the first time since I heard the news. She added, "Your dad died the next day. They didn't find him until three days later." "Oh no," I thought, "My dad came to find me. I wasn't there! He died without ever telling me he was sorry for hurting me. I was sick to my stomach. I slept on the sofa that night at my sisters' house. I kept thinking, "I forgive you dad, please forgive me."

It was time for the funeral. Once again I'm in the middle of a snowstorm in Pennsylvania. I was so happy to get it over with so I could be on my way. I loved my father; I believe he loved me. He just didn't know how to show it.

I was happy to be on the bus back to Kansas. I left about five o'clock in the afternoon. I arrived at the Cleveland bus terminal nearly two hours later. It was dark outside, still snowing quite heavily. I started feeling very strange as I got off the bus entering the terminal. I didn't know what was going on, I had a horrible fear come over me. The lay over there was about an hour so I kept trying to calm myself down. I felt numb; my heart was racing like I was going to have a heart attack. I tried to think on other things. The rest of the trip was a nightmare. Jimmie and Dan picked me up at the bus station when I arrived back home that Friday morning. "I have to see a doctor, something is wrong with me," I told Jimmie as I opened the car door. I was so happy to see Daniel; he was the only thing in my life that made sense to me. "What's wrong Christine?" Jimmie asked me. I could hardly describe what I was feeling. "I feel very strange," I told him, "I just need to see a doctor right away."

Jimmie didn't have much to say on the ride home. I ran into the house to call Dr. Burns office. My hands were shaking; I felt horrible. I was tired from lack of sleep. I couldn't eat! Dr. Burns agreed to work me in that afternoon. I arrived at the doctors' office a couple hours later. A nurse took me back to a waiting room. "Dr. Burns will be with you shortly," she said. I sat in that little room for what seemed like an eternity. I kept thinking about the things going on in my life. "I've lost two babies, Janet, and my dad is gone forever," I thought. "What's going on with you Christine?" Dr. Burns asked as he walked in to the room. I began to tell him about my trip back from my father's funeral. "I feel afraid, my heart races, almost like something bad is going to happen," I told him. As I sat there and heard the words come out of my mouth, it sounded so crazy. He had a puzzled look on his face as he told me, "Sometimes we don't like to face the things that have happened to us, we want to lock them up somewhere in the back of our mind." I just sat there bewildered. "Am I crazy?" I thought.

"What you're experiencing could be a chemical imbalance or it could be an anxiety attack," he added. We sat in his office talking for a while. He was sure this would pass but that I could feel free to call him at anytime. When I left the doctors' office that afternoon I felt better but the anxiety attack was still with me. The only way I could describe it to Jimmie was, "I feel panicked." The next several days were the darkest days of my life. I couldn't eat, or sleep! I cried most of the time. I went to see Dr. Burns several times over the next few weeks. We would sit and talk. Sometimes the attacks were bad. Other times, I felt as though there were a dark cloud hanging over my head. Life got easier as time went by. I really appreciated Dr. Burns. He never gave me medication for my problem. In his own way, he made me deal with the issues in my life. I had a Living Bible that Brian's mom had given us when we were married. I would read it from time to time. There was peace and comfort in doing that.

DO YOU KNOW GOD

The next couple of years went by rather quickly. I graduated from Beauty College and started work at a local salon. Jimmie and I were not getting along very well. It was me. Jimmie didn't like for us to go out much into public. People always stared at us, being a bi-racial couple. Having Dan made it even worse. He was growing up so fast! Jimmie and I fought constantly. I hated our life. I didn't care what people thought but Jimmie did. I felt bad about Dan not having his father around. Brian didn't make any efforts to see his son. I knew deep down Jimmie was right about our mixed up family. I would convince myself that it was time to leave Jimmie, and then talk myself out of it.

It was the fall of 1982 we got the news that I was pregnant again. Jimmie's drinking was getting out of hand but we decided to make this work since we were going to have a baby. I was scared to say the least. My mother's words haunted me once again, "God doesn't want you to have this baby." I kept telling myself, "I'm going to have this baby, no matter what." I got off to a bad start. I was very sick with morning sickness. I gained a lot of weight. Into my seventh month we started rejoicing. If I went into labor now, the baby had more of a chance of survival.

The end of July 1983, Marcus was born. I had a rough time during the delivery but we made it. I heard the doctor say, "Give him oxygen, he's not breathing." I remembered thinking, "No! Don't take this baby!" Then I heard my newborn baby cry for the first time. I was so relieved. "Thank you Lord," I whispered. "He looks just like me," I heard Jimmie say. Marcus was fine.

I was miserable for the next couple of years. Jimmie and I didn't get along at all. I didn't love him anymore. I was fed up with the way he treated me. His drinking had gotten worse and it pushed me further and further away from him. I left him a couple of times but always came back home. I felt so guilty because I didn't want to take Marc's dad away from him. I knew Dan would someday want answers about his father. I also knew deep down in my heart I wasn't spending the rest of my life with Jimmie.

Jimmie came home one afternoon as I was packing bags to leave. "I got a new job in the city. I'm leaving you," I told him. "I'll be back for the rest of my things in a few days," I said as I was trying to hurry out the door. I knew that if I stayed for long he would talk me out of it again. This time I was leaving for sure. Daniel was upset that we were leaving his dad. Jimmie was the only father he knew. This was something I felt I had to do.

Dan, Marcus and I got moved into our new apartment. I got a job right down the street. I got Daniel into his new school and Marc into a day care. Marc was now three years old. Jimmie was still doing the same old things. He did come by to see the boys a lot, which I appreciated. I filed for divorce from Jimmie. He didn't take it well but we tried to get along for the boys sake. I had a good job! I had my boys! But I still had a void in my life.

I remember being at work one hot afternoon in September of 1986. Our salon was very busy that day. I went up to take the next customer for a haircut. He was a middle-aged man in a very nice suit. He was reading his mail as I tried to start a conversation with him. Looking up from reading his mail he asked me, "Do you know God?" I said, "Yes, I do." I was taken by surprise at his question. "He must be a preacher or something," I thought. Still looking up at me he asked again, "Do you really know God?"

I glared at him because he obviously did not believe me the first time he asked. He then told me that he pastored a little church downtown. We didn't talk much after that, I hurried with the haircut and sent him on his way. That night I couldn't get that preacher off my mind. I kept hearing those words, "Do you know God?" I thought, "Of course I know God, I have a bible. I asked Jesus into my heart as a child." Even though I didn't attend church, I still took Dan to a small Baptist church in our neighborhood for Sunday school.

My court date for my divorce from Jimmie was scheduled for September 10, 1986. He didn't contest it so I knew it would be over soon. He would still come by to see us. I knew how much Marcus meant to him. Marcus was such an entertainer. He loved to sing and dance. We used to say, "Marcus is going to grow up to a singer." He was so precious. I used to love watching Daniel and Marcus together. Marcus loved his big brother. At night after the boys were asleep I would find myself reading from the Living Bible that Brian's mom gave us years ago. It was starting to look a little beat up, but I still loved that book.

Times were hard for the boys and me. I was barely making enough for us to live on. If it weren't for the tips I made everyday at work from my haircuts, I don't know how I would have fed the boys. I walked to work as much as I could because I couldn't afford the gas in my old car. We only lived a few blocks from the salon, so it wasn't so bad. Daniel would get frustrated because I couldn't afford things that he wanted. It was all I could do to survive. All of our clothes were second hand. I would go to yard sales for our furnishings. It bothered me that I couldn't do more for the boys but I was content with what we did have.

It came time for my divorce hearing. It was like I thought it would be. I was in there for about ten minutes. Jimmie and I had decided on joint custody of Marcus so I didn't request child support. Jimmie wasn't working much in those days so

I left it alone. He promised to help me out with Marc's day care. I settled for that; doubting that I'd ever get anything.

I was finally divorced! I kept trying to get on with my life. I was hurting so much inside. I didn't know what I wanted to do. I had the boys to take care of. I really had no friends or family. I was so miserable; so was Jimmie. I wanted him to get on with his life but he spent most of his time with us. I didn't care; I just knew I didn't have to answer to him ever again.

I kept thinking about the preacher that came into the salon that day. I didn't know why but I kept asking myself, "Do I know God?" I was sure that I did, but I was in no way prepared for what was about to happen that Thursday afternoon, September 11, 1986.

THE TRACHEOTOMY

As I sat in the hospital waiting room with David that night, I looked at my life up to this point. "Nothing makes sense in my life," I told him as I started to cry again. I made Jesus the Lord of my life. I wanted answers. Why was all of this happening to us? What was going to become of Marcus? Was I going to be able to care for him? I talked to David that night and shared some of my frustrations. "Have you thought about attending church Christine?" David asked me. Going to church at that time was the last thing I wanted to do. "I have thought about it, but I don't know where to start looking for one," I told him. "I know of a couple of good ones around here, let me know if you're interested," he said. David prayed with me before he left that night. Marcus was still in the intensive care unit fighting for his life. I could do nothing to help him. I put the thought of going to church on the back burner.

While we were staying at the hospital, Jimmie would get Dan to and from school. He met a couple of boys that lived behind us. They didn't go to school with Dan because they were home schooled. He was so excited to have made new friends. "Guess what Mom?" he said. "They go to church. They invited me to go with them tomorrow night! Their mom is the children's church worker, can I go?" he asked. I could see the excitement in his eyes as I said, "I guess you can, but Jimmie needs to meet their mom." Jimmie got Dan after school the next day and they went over to the boy's house to meet their mother. Jimmie let Dan go to church with them and when he got home they came back to the hospital. Daniel was so excited, "Mom, this church is so fun!" he told me. "You should go with me, can I go back?

They go on Sunday mornings and Sunday nights." I still had no desire to go, but I agreed that he could go with them.

I was still a mess; my baby was still in a coma. Everything that could go wrong did. Marc was still on a ventilator. He got pneumonia so they were treating that. I'll never forget this one night. They had to move Marc's bed to an adjoining room to accommodate a child who needed to be in isolation. In the process of moving him; his ventilator tube came out. I was petrified! Jimmie and I stood there as the nurse was trying to get it back in his throat. She couldn't get the ventilator tube back in his airway passage. I panicked and Jimmie made me leave the room. The nurse finally called the doctor and he told her to leave it out to see how he does breathing on his own. What a horrible night it was! Jimmie and I sat there watching Marcus fight for every breath he took. We finally told the nurse to do something. I thought he was going to die right there. She finally called the doctor back and he told her to get him reintubated. The next morning we met Dr. Henry as he came in to check on Marc. "Marc needs to get off the ventilator so I am calling in an ENT (ear, nose, and throat doctor)," He told us. "Dr. Warner will do a tracheotomy. That will enable us to give his airway passage a rest." I was so tired and really concerned about the doctor doing a tracheotomy on Marcus. Dr. Warner came to see us that afternoon. He went in and examined Marc, then came to talk to Jimmie and me. "There is a lot of swelling in Marc's airway passage. I will do the tracheotomy today. I will come back in a few days to see how he is doing," he explained. He went on to say, "As soon as the swelling goes down, we will be able to take the trach out." The nurses got Marc ready to go to surgery. It was about an hour surgery so Jimmie and I waited in our room.

I was still in shock over all of this. It wasn't long they brought Marc back to the intensive care unit. "Everything went fine," Dr. Warner told us. "I'll be back in a few days to check on him!" Jimmie and I went in to see Marc. He had the tracheotomy in his throat. We watched the nurses as they cared for the trach.

We could hear a gurgling sound as Marc was breathing. The nurse would proceed to suction the trach. It nauseated me to watch what she was doing. She had a suction catheter that had long skinny tubing on it that she stuck down in the trach. It would suction mucus out of his lungs. Marcus would cough every time she stuck that catheter in the trach. They had a small plastic mask with an elastic strap that fit around his neck. The mask had plastic tubing that ran to a humidifier. The humidity was to keep the mucus moist, making it easier for him to cough it out.

I looked for David that night and sure enough he came to visit. We sat across the hall in our little room. I was always so happy to see him. It was a reminder to me that every thing was going to be all right. He was teaching me things about God. The encouragement I got from him was awesome. I always felt like I could take on the whole world after his visits. I drew strength from him. Everyday I thanked God for David's visits. "Daniel has been going to church with our neighbors," I told him. "He really likes it there." I knew what David was going to say next, "Have you considered going yourself Christine?" I knew I needed to go. I couldn't stop thinking about it. "It's called, Light of the World Christian Center," I told him. "I may visit on Sunday morning." David smiled as he said, "You should go; you will enjoy it!"

Jimmie and I had a lot of other problems we were being faced with. Even my rent was hard to pay. I saw Jimmie moving back into our lives. I didn't want it, but I realized this wasn't about me. We had to stick together for Marcus' sake. I was determined to take my baby home. Every day was a promising day with Marcus. I would talk to him while rubbing his feet. Sometimes he would smile and other times there would be tears. I would look at him and think, "Where is he? Does he really know I am here?" I just knew that I wanted my baby back.

The nurses said his brain damage was so severe; it was hard to know if he would ever come out of the coma. If he did come out, what would he be like?

It was five days later they took Marc back to surgery to remove the trach. I was more than ready for that thing to be gone. The next thing I knew Dr. Warner came to see us. "Can I talk to you both out in the hall?" he asked Jimmie and me. We walked out to the hallway. I was feeling sick to my stomach. Something was wrong, terribly wrong! His words felt like a knife going into my back, "I'm not able to take the trach out." He said. "I've looked down into the airway passage. It is closed with scar tissue. It was like I ran into a brick wall down there." I started to cry as I heard him say, "I'm sorry, there is nothing I can do." I ran into our room. I was so sick of hearing those words. Once again I found myself talking to God, "Why are you doing this? I can't take anymore!" My mind was running in all different directions. What kind of future could Marcus possibly have? He couldn't make a sound. He had to depend on this trach to breathe. I was devastated! David came to see us that night. We gave him the doctor's report. He prayed with us for Marcus. "God will turn this around!" he said. After talking with David that night, I realized that we had to be grateful for what we did have. Marcus was still alive!

It was a Sunday morning that first week of October. I decided it was time for me to go to church. I needed some time away from the hospital; not to mention that curiosity had the best of me. Dan loved this church and had been attending regularly with our neighbors since his first visit. I went home, showered, and put on my Sunday best. I pulled into the parking lot, looking for an out of the way spot. I sat in my car crying for over an hour. I couldn't get out of the car. I was hurting so bad. I felt that everything bad in my life was all God's fault. Even though David was teaching me about God, I never saw myself being close to him.

I didn't know why I was there. I could never be a Godly person; I just wanted him to keep Marcus alive. I wanted Marcus back to normal.

I left the parking lot frustrated with myself. I drove back to the hospital trying to convince myself to go back again. "Did you like the church?" Jimmie asked when I walked into Marc's room. "I didn't go in, I think I'll go back tonight," I told him. Jimmie just shook his head. I didn't know why I wanted to go back; I couldn't explain it. I felt like I needed to go. Even if I just sat in the parking lot, I felt better. That night I arrived at the church and I decided to go in. I knew Dan was in there and I told myself, "Go on, if you don't like it, leave." I remember hearing music as I opened the door. A woman who extended her hand to me greeted me with a warm smile. "Welcome! It's nice to see you." She said. I went on in but stood at the back row while all these people were singing and praising God. I stood there in awe; I'd never seen anything like this.

When the pastor said we could take our seats, I looked around the congregation. So many people packed into this sanctuary. I could immediately tell the pastor was a man who loved God. He kept saying Hallelujah and Amen! Tears were burning my eyes. As he shared the Word of God, I felt things happening to me. I brought the little black bible with the zipper that my grandmother gave me back in 1963. The pastor said to open your bible to John 10:10. I was so anxious to find it I was fumbling. He began to read the scripture, "The thief cometh not, but for to steal, kill, and to destroy: I am come that they might have life, and that they might have it more abundantly." He continued to say, "People blame God for every bad thing that happens in their lives. We have an enemy!" He then took us to I Peter 5:8 and read, "Be sober, be vigilant, because your adversary, the devil, as a roaring lion, walketh about, seeking whom he may devour." It was as though a light came on inside of me. Here I was, thirty years old, and these two scriptures changed the way I looked at God in an instant. All my life I thought God was beating me to death. I was so excited! I was born again so the bible says I have an enemy. The service came to an end. I didn't want it to be over. However, I was the first one out the door; I didn't want to talk to anyone.

I could hardly wait for the following Wednesday night. I was going back to church. Dan was excited that I would be driving him from now on. Jimmie wouldn't go but I felt there was something there that I needed more of. When I walked in the door that feeling came over me once again. It was an inner peace, like I belonged there. Dan told me the pastors' name was Greg Varney. I sat at the back of the church once again listening to another awesome message. "We are God's children, he loves us; he died for us," Pastor Greg said. I remember thinking how much I loved my own children. He was saying how much more our Heavenly Father loved us. Wow! My father! I've never heard anything like this. "Turn in your bibles to Matthew 7:11," Pastor Greg said. He read as Jesus spoke, "If ye then, being evil, know how to give good gifts unto your children, how much more shall your father which is in heaven give good things to them that ask him?" I couldn't believe what I was hearing! It wasn't God who was trying to kill Marcus, the devil was. I learned that God cared about me, he loved me, and that when I prayed, he heard me. God desired good things for my life, not bad things.

After the service I ran out that door not wanting to be confronted by anyone. As I approached my car I heard a voice behind me, "Sister?" I turned around to see the pastor standing there. "You left so fast the other night I didn't get to meet you," he said. "I'm Pastor Varney." I shook his hand. "We'd like for you to come back again," he told me. I opened my car door as I told him, "I'll be back!

I really enjoy the services here." The moment Dan and I arrived back at the hospital, reality set back in. Marcus was still in the coma with a tracheotomy. However, I was beginning to look at life a little differently. I wasn't as angry with God as I had been all my life. I knew I had a long way to go with a rough road ahead of me. The inner peace I was feeling was indescribable. I continued to go to church. David kept stopping by the hospital to see us. I got so hungry for the Word of God. I couldn't get enough of it. There were so many things I didn't understand. At the church, during their praise and worship time, they were singing in tongues. I never heard anything like it. But, I kept going back for more. It was awesome! Once inside those doors, I felt like a new person. All of the pain, problems, and issues in my life seemed so unimportant. I would stand in church crying like a baby. After each church service I'd leave with an inner strength that I didn't know I had.

One Sunday morning toward the end of the service I heard Pastor Greg say, "Christine, could you come up here? The Lord wants me to pray for you." I ran to the front of the church! "Yes Lord, I want what you have for me," I whispered. I never had someone pray for me like this. I stretched my hands toward heaven as he prayed. The tears rolled down my cheeks as I literally felt the warm healing power of the Holy Spirit flood my heart. That is where the pain was! An enormous amount of hate, guilt, shame, hurt; ugly stuff that God had to get out of there. I knew at that moment I would never be the same person on the inside. That day I gave my family, my childhood, everything to the Lord. I wanted this healing.

It was time for me to call mom. I called her right after the accident to let her know about Marcus. She didn't have much to say at that time. Mom had started going to church with a couple of my sisters.

I wanted her to know that I gave my life to Jesus. I was attending a great church! "This church is so wonderful mom," I told her. "They have awesome praise and worship. They also pray in tongues," I said. I didn't pray in tongues. I didn't know enough about it, yet! "You need to get out of there, that stuff is of the devil," she warned me. Oh no, here we go again. "No mom, I know there are scriptures about it, it's not from the devil!" I explained. I knew that I wasn't going to be able to change her mind. Once again I was disappointed. I had hoped that she would be happy for me, but she wasn't. I was changing on the inside so I wasn't about to give it up for anyone.

I knew that it was about time for me to learn how to pray. I was giving it my best but I was learning there were different ways to pray. The church announced a teaching series on how to pray. I was so excited! It was a week long study that took place in the evening. It was perfect because it was hard for me to be gone from the hospital during the day. Jimmie and Dan would get to the hospital around dinnertime. I would then be able to attend the class while Jimmie stayed with Marcus. I needed this class badly! I still wasn't praying in tongues but I knew I was saved. I wanted to communicate better with God.

The class started on a Monday night. The teaching covered the Lord's Prayer in the book of Matthew, chapter six. I knew the Lord's Prayer from a long time ago. It was hanging on the wall in my grandmothers' house. In verse nine it says, "Our Father which art in heaven, hallowed be thy name." That was acknowledging God, and giving him praise for who he is. In verse ten we are praying for his will to be done in our lives. In verse eleven it says, "Give us this day, our daily bread." This is where we tell the Lord of our needs. We lay our petition at his feet. Verse twelve says, "And forgive us our debts, as we forgive our debtors."

I learned that we needed forgiveness from God, but that God also expects us to forgive those who hurt us. Verse thirteen says, "And lead us not into temptation, but deliver us from evil." I now pray for God's protection over me and my family, he delivers us from evil. The last part of that verse says, "For thine is the kingdom, and the power, and the glory, for ever. At the end of my prayer, I thank him and give him praise for doing the things I have asked of him.

I enjoyed this class so much. Communicating with God is a vital part of our everyday life. I was depending on David to pray for Marc and my family. I finally had the confidence that I needed to know that God wanted me to be the praying person. I could hardly believe how our lives have changed from Marc's accident. I still remember the day that the pastor came into the salon and asked me, "Do you know God?" I didn't know God, not at all! I knew of him; I believed in his existence, but I didn't know him. One thing I know now, that pastor planted a seed in my heart that day. I longed to know God, but I felt that he was out of my reach.

How wonderful to know that I could get with God one on one.

GOING HOME

Amazing things were happening over the next few weeks at the hospital. Dr. Warner came back to see us one afternoon and said, "I've talked with a doctor in Chicago who specializes in pediatric throat surgeries. There is a procedure that we can try on Marcus to open his airway." Jimmie was a bit apprehensive but I listened anyway. "I can laser and dilate the scar tissue that is in the larynx over the next couple of weeks. I will then put a plastic stint in place for a few days. It may heal around that stint giving him an airway." Dr. Warner added. Jimmie and I agreed so he started the procedures.

The holidays were approaching. We were still living at the hospital. I'll never forget this one night; Dr. Warner had ordered a throat scan for a surgery the next morning. Marcus seemed to be agitated that afternoon. After dinner they took him down to x-ray. "I'll go down there with him Christine, you wait up here," Jimmie told me as they were taking Marc's bed down the hallway towards the elevator. After about an hour I was getting anxious. "Does it normally take this long for an x-ray?" I asked one of the nurses at the station. "No, it doesn't, I will call down there and see what is going on," she told me. I listened as she was talking to the x-ray department on the phone. "Marcus is moving around a lot. They are having a hard time getting him to lie still to get the x-ray of his throat." She told me as she was hanging up the phone. I started to pace the floor. "Why is he moving around so much?" I thought. "What is happening?" Another hour or so went by. Jimmie finally came back up to the fifth floor where I was walking the halls. "What happened down there?" I asked him. "I'm not sure but I think Marcus is coming out of the coma," he said.

"I've never seen anything like it Christine, Marcus was throwing his arms and legs everywhere. They ended up giving him some tranquilizers to calm him down but they didn't work." He added. I couldn't believe what I was hearing. I was afraid, but excited at the same time, that Marcus could be coming out of the coma. "They finally had to call in an anesthesiologist to put him to sleep so they could get the x-ray," Jimmie told me. We sat in our room waiting for them to bring Marcus back up to the fifth floor that night. I couldn't wait to see him. He was asleep when they finally arrived but not for long. It was a long night. Thank God, our little Marcus was coming out of the coma.

The next day, Marcus was wide-awake, moving around a lot. His eyes were open, but they were still looking straight ahead. He developed a rash so they moved us out of intensive care. We were moved into a private room for isolation. I'll never forget that day. I had a rocking chair sitting by Marc's bed. The nurse let me hold him. It was so wonderful holding him. I had to support his head because he couldn't hold it up yet. He felt like such a big boy sitting in my lap but at the same time, like a newborn baby. I sat there rocking in that chair holding my little boy in my arms thinking, "If it had not been for that man David, knowing God like he did, Marcus and I would have died that first week in the hospital."

We still had a long road ahead of us. As the days went by, Marc's eyes were starting to focus on us. They would follow us around the room. The nurses brought us some ice cream to feed Marc one day. "We have to start him out on soft foods to see if he can swallow," the nurse told me. It was exciting to see Marc eat the ice cream. She brought in jars of baby food for me to feed him. After that, they took him off the feeding tube and we were able to feed him.

I was more than glad to get rid of the feeding tube but we still had the IV. I hated the IV's because it was as though every other day they would go bad. Every time they had to put in a new IV, I'd get upset. He would cry; I'd leave the room. It hurt me so bad to see the tears roll down his face but not be able to hear a sound.

One night I waited at the nurses' station while they were replacing Marc's IV. One of the nurses told me, "We are so happy for you and your family." She then said, "We really didn't think that little boy was going to make it. None of us wanted to be the one to have to tell you when he died." We talked about being parents as I asked her, "Where are these other babies' moms?" I would walk the halls at night; seeing nurses rocking little children to sleep. I couldn't understand why there were no parents there with these children. "The children get sick, and then brought to the hospital," she said. "Sometimes we don't see parents again until its time for the child to go home." I thought, "How sad that is." When I think of all that we had been through with Marcus and how we would have gladly given our life for his, I couldn't comprehend these children being hospitalized without their parents by their side. The entire time we spent at the hospital, Jimmie and I could feel Marc's pain. We desperately wanted to take it from him.

Thanksgiving came and went; Big Mama came to spend some time with us. What an awesome lady she was. She was the mother I never had! Big Mama was so good to me and I loved her dearly. Marcus was doing really well by this time. We were still at the hospital because of all of the surgeries they were performing on Marc's throat. I thanked God for him! Marcus could see, he could hear, and he also could use his legs. The nurses brought us a walker for him to use. Marcus would take off down the hall just as fast as his little legs could go. "Amazing Lord," I would say quietly as I watched him.

Jimmie, Big Mama and I sat in Marc's room one evening watching him sleep. "We should be able to take him home soon Christine." Jimmie said. "I think we should talk to the doctor tomorrow." I agreed, "Yes, but I'm not sure if I can handle his trach." I was petrified at the thought of caring for Marc's trach. Anytime they came in the room to do anything with the trach I went running out. I knew if my child was going to have it for any amount of time I had to get used to it.

The next morning Dr. Henry came by to see Marcus. "We would like to take Marc home." I heard Jimmie tell him. "Christmas is less than two weeks away, we'd all love to be home by then," he added. Dr. Henry looked at both of us, "I think that's a terrific idea. Let's get you both in our trach care classes. You'll also need to complete CPR training. Then you can take Marc home." I wasn't looking forward to these classes. We've been here three months. It was time to go home!

The first thing I had to do was get the fear of this trach under control. David came to see us later that week. "David, we are taking Marc home, can you believe it?" I said. David smiled at me. "I never doubted it for one minute." He said. I knew that David heard from the Lord. He knew all along Marcus would be going home one day.

It wasn't long before they had us in classes on trach care. The nurses were wonderful in getting us in touch with a local medical supply company who got us everything we would need for Marc's homecoming. Christmas Eve finally came! We were more than ready to go. Jimmie and Daniel sat in Marc's room as I paced the floor. We were waiting on the release from the doctor. After dinner the nurse finally came in, "Here are the release papers for you to sign, you can take Marcus home," she said. I can't really put into words how we felt that night.

Three and a half months we lived at this hospital. Three and a half months ago they told me my baby was going to die! Marcus was alive and well! Jimmie and I had a lot to be grateful for. It was a rough time in our lives that we would never forget. I know that it was the grace of God that brought us through.

It was so good to be home! It was the best Christmas anyone could ever hope for. Marcus was walking now. Money was so tight we didn't have much under the tree. Dan and Marcus were just glad to be at home. I was still going to church. I had so much yet to learn. I wanted to go back to work but I knew it would be hard to find someone to take care of Marc. I thanked God for the medical card we had to take care of Marc's needs.

About two weeks after we got home a gentleman from an insurance company came to see me. The woman that hit Marc had an insurance policy that would pay Marc one hundred fifty thousand dollars to help with medical expenses. I was excited since we had to be planning for our trip to Chicago to meet with the doctor that may be able to help Marc. We had no money. "You will need to get an attorney to set him up a fund," he told me. "Call me when you have that set up." When Jimmie got home from work that night I could hardly wait to tell him the news. Jimmie made an appointment with a lawyer that agreed to meet with us. Jimmie and I like him so we hired him to be the executor of Marcus' trust fund.

Meanwhile Marc was still having one, sometimes two minor surgeries a week while we were waiting to get in to see the doctor in Chicago. I notified the state that Marcus now had the trust fund. They immediately stopped the medical benefits he was receiving. Now the doctors, anesthesiologist, even the medical supply company were all sending the bills to the attorneys' office for payment.

The doctors' office in Chicago finally called us. Marcus was scheduled for an exploratory surgery. It was impossible for us all to make the trip so we agreed Jimmie would take him. The doctor would do the examination; then let us know if there was anything he could do. Dan and I stayed home anxious to hear the news. "This surgeon is awesome Christine," Jimmie told me as he walked in the door carrying Marcus. "There is a procedure they can do on Marc, its reconstructive surgery." I could tell Jimmie felt really good about this doctor because he was talking so fast. "He will use Marc's rib cartilage to create him a new airway," he said. I looked at him in amazement, "Can they really do that?" I asked him. "This doctor is going to try, but he can't guarantee anything," he said. Jimmie went on to tell me, "It is an eight hour surgery Christine! We are going back in a few months for about three weeks." I didn't want to do this. I didn't want to put Marcus through an eight-hour surgery. I just got him home. I wanted to keep him home.

Every night I prayed, "God, why does Marc still have this trach? I saw you heal him from a twisted brain stem. Please take this trach." I didn't understand but I knew a scripture very well that said, "Trust in the Lord with all your heart, lean not unto your own understanding." (Proverbs 3:5)

It was February of 1987. Hard times were all around us. We could hardly afford to buy food. Marc's money was tied up in this fund. It angered Jimmie that we couldn't at least invest some of it for Marc's future. It was going towards medical expenses, disappearing fast. I was spending about three hundred dollars a month just for medical supplies that we had to have at home for Marc's trach. And the minor surgeries still being done were costing nearly two thousand dollars each. I hated this trach with a passion. Every time Marc would cough, my heart would stop. I still had a horrible fear of it.

Marcus had a humidifier that he spent a lot of time on. The humidifier was a small machine that a nebulizer attached to. The nebulizer had a container that screwed to the bottom of it that held sterile water. The hose, or tubing, attached to the nebulizer. It had a small plastic mask on the end of it that we would tie around his neck.

Marc also had a suction machine. He would need suctioned several times a day. I could always tell when he needed suctioned because his breathing would always change. He would sound congested. I would place a few drops of saline in the trach; this would make him cough. I would then slide the suction catheter down in to the trach tube until I could feel the end of the tube. The catheter would remove secretions from the trach tube and help clear his lungs. The trach tube could get blocked with mucus or even blood clots. Humidifying, along with suctioning would prevent blockage. I took Marcus in to see Dr. Warner about once a week to get his trach changed. Jimmie and I were not shown how to do that nor did I want any part of it.

Jimmie was attending church with me once in a while. I enjoyed taking the boys. If Jimmie didn't go, I would just take Dan with me. Marcus would stay home with his dad. I loved church! I didn't know how I was dealing with the issues in our lives, I just was. I still enjoyed my conversations with David. I would call him when I had questions. He would stop by from time to time to see how we were doing. I would always give him my prayer requests.

One Sunday night at church I decided it was time for me to receive the baptism in the Holy Spirit. I had been around it for several months now. I studied the scriptures. I knew it was for all believers in Christ. I was so excited! I couldn't wait to get home that night to call David. He worked at night for the railroad. I would call him there.

I got a different man on the phone that night. "Could I please speak to David?" I asked. "I'm sorry but David isn't working tonight, he is in the hospital!" The man told me. I felt fear sweep over me. I felt sick to my stomach as I called the hospital. A nurse put my call through to David's room. I was so happy to hear his voice, "What happened, why are you there?" I asked him. His voice sounded weak as he said, "It was a heart attack, don't worry, just the devil giving me a hard time." I wanted to cry right there. "They are doing a by-pass surgery tomorrow afternoon," he said. I was worried about him. "Marc and I will be there to see you in the morning," I told him. David assured me he was going to be fine.

The next morning Marc and I arrived at the hospital around ten o'clock. David's' bed was empty. A nurse came in the room to tell us, "They took him to surgery about an hour ago." I walked out of that room fighting my tears. Marcus and I went home. I prayed! I told God that I needed David in my life. It was a long day; I called the hospital every couple of hours. They continued to tell me he was still in surgery. My last call was about ten o'clock that night. Twelve hours David had been in surgery. I finally fell asleep. I woke the next morning about six thirty. I couldn't wait to call the hospital. I was anxious to see how David was doing. I got a nurse on the phone and she asked me, "Are you a relative?" I told her, "No, I'm a close friend; I'm very worried about him." She asked, "Are you the lady that called all day yesterday?" I assured her that I was. She proceeded to tell me, "David never came out of the surgery, I'm so sorry." I couldn't believe this was happening to me! "Dear God, why are you doing this to me again?" I cried as I hung up the phone.

David was like a brother to me. I hurt badly when I lost Joe at the age of thirteen. I never thought there would be another Joe in my life. Then God gave me David.

I had to keep reminding myself that David went home to be with the Lord. I felt so alone at first. I had no one to call when I needed something. I was on my own. After some time went by I realized it was time for me to grow up in the things of the Lord. I knew I was in good hands; the Lord said he would never leave me or forsake me.

RECONSTRUCTIVE SURGERY

Marcus turned four the summer of 1987. I was so amazed at him. It was almost time for the major surgery in Chicago. I was anxious to meet this doctor Jimmie was so impressed with. Dr. Foster was referred to us as the best pediatric otolaryngologist in the country. I was still praying for this trach to be gone. It was September of 1987 when we arrived in Chicago. Large cities made me nervous. We found our way to the Children's Hospital. Jimmie got Marc checked in. A nurse took him to an examination room. He was scheduled for surgery the next day. The hospital put us up in a large waiting area with other family members of children that were in the hospital. They assigned us a locker for our personal belongings and three fold up cots to sleep on.

I was more than ready for the next morning to get here. It was a long night, sleeping in a room full of strange people. Morning finally came. They took Marc back for the surgery. I had the privilege of meeting Dr. Foster at that time. I had to admit that I was also very impressed. Dr. Foster explained the procedure he was going to do on Marcus. "I will be using rib cartilage from Marcus to form a new airway. I will insert a metal stint that will be attached to a metal trach," he said. "I will then run a wire to the inside of his nose that will be attached to the stint also." He continued. "How are we supposed to change his trach?" Jimmie asked. Dr. Foster went on to say, "You won't be able to take the trach out for any reason; it will have an inner canula in it that you can remove for cleaning purposes." I was not looking forward to this at all. I wanted to wake up from this nightmare I had been in for the last year. "This surgery will probably take about eight hours to complete," Dr. Foster said as he left Jimmie and I sitting in the waiting room.

It was one of the longest days of my life. A nurse finally came to get Jimmie and me. We followed her down a corridor to a small room. "You can wait in here; the doctor will be with you shortly." She said pointing to a small table with four chairs around it. Five minutes later Dr. Foster came in. "The surgery went very well; Marcus is doing fine," he said. "They just took him in to the recovery room. He will be moved to the intensive care unit where he will be for a week to ten days," he added. "At that time they will be weaning him off a paralyzing drug we use to stabilize him during the reconstruction. It is very important that he not be able to move his body during this critical time. I have the stint in place in the airway." I hated that Marcus had to go through all of this.

Dr. Foster went on to say, "You will be able to take him home in a few weeks, and then you need to bring him back in about six months. I will remove the stint at that time. Let's hope the airway has healed around the stint, if so, we will be able to remove the trach." I felt so bad for Marcus. Seeing him get weaned off the paralyzing drug was awful. His little body looked like he was convulsing. I would see tears roll down his face. It took what seemed like forever but we made it. We finally got to take Marcus home.

Our hope now was that the new airway would remain open when they removed the stint in six months. I spent a lot of time in prayer. I studied God's Word in hopes of the manifestation of this healing we were so desperately seeking. I kept clinging to David's words, "He'll not have this trach forever."

The next few months were very trying for me. Many times I wanted to run away. I wanted to hide myself from the rest of the world. I knew if Jimmie and I were going to make it he would have to give up his drinking.

The closer I got to God, the more he would drink. After a couple of months being home from Chicago, Big Mama came to spend a few days with us. Big Mama would tell me, "Don't fight with him; pray that God will take the desire for the liquor away from him." I loved her faith in the Lord. "You don't know what it's like living with him, Mama." I said, "He wants to argue with me all the time. I'm so tired of it!" Deep down I knew I wanted to leave this man but I sincerely did not have the strength left in me to do it.

I didn't think I did, but I left Jimmie in the spring of 1988. I was having a hard time going to church, praying, even believing God for anything. I felt as though my prayers were going unanswered. Marcus was out of money in his trust fund. I had to depend on the state again for his medical needs. I worked but barely made ends meet. Childcare was so hard to find, not many people wanted to take care of a child with a trach.

I remember it being a really warm day in June of 1988; Daniel played on a little league ball team and we had a game that afternoon. As I drove Dan to his game I noticed Marcus' breathing was sounding rough. It was a hot day so I decided to drop Dan off at his game. I wanted to take Marcus back home to put him on his humidifier. When we arrived at the ball field I told him, "Your brother needs to be on his humidifier, I'm going to take him back home." Dan took off running towards the field. Marcus and I headed for home. As I was driving I could hear Marcus breathing really hard. I looked over at him sitting in the seat beside me; blood everywhere, all over his neck and shirt. I panicked; now heading for the nearest hospital. I got him in to the emergency room. They immediately started to suction him. "Where did he get this trach?" a doctor asked me as he was putting Marc on humidity. "We had surgery in Chicago a few months ago. This trach is a result of that surgery." I explained. The look on this doctor's face worried me.

"Dr. Foster in Chicago is Marc's doctor," I said. We agreed he should get him on the phone. I stood there beside Marc's bed. The bleeding seemed to lessen. "I just spoke to Dr. Foster in Chicago," the emergency room doctor said as he came back in the room. "Keep Marc suctioned and on very warm humidity; if the bleeding persists or gets worse, Dr. Foster wants you to call your local ear, nose, and throat doctor." He continued. I agreed. We stayed at the hospital for about another thirty minutes on the humidifier. It was time to get Dan from his ball game so we left.

The boys and I arrived home a short while later. I put Marc on his humidifier. After a couple hours the bleeding started up again. I kept suctioning him while he was on the humidifier. I didn't know what else to do. I put a call in to Dr. Warner. He knew Marc's history. He had taken care of him from the beginning. I called his answering service, "Could you please have Dr. Warner call me, this is an emergency." I left my name and number. I couldn't understand why Dr. Warner wasn't calling me back. I waited for an hour before calling the answering service again. They assured me that he would call me soon. In the meantime I kept suctioning Marc and kept the humidity warm. Another hour went by, I began to cry. I called the answering service. "I don't know why Dr. Warner has not called you; I've given him both of your messages." His answering service told me. "I will page him again." I was almost hysterical, I was so afraid for Marcus. The phone finally rang, it was Dr. Warner, "There isn't anything more I can do for you or Marcus," he told me. I was in shock; I couldn't believe what I was hearing! That was it! He hung up! Tears burned my eyes as I looked for my phone book to call Dr. Foster in Chicago. I had to do something! After the call to Dr. Foster's answering service I just sat there waiting for the phone to ring. I remembered thinking, "Am I going to have to move to

Chicago to be around a doctor that can take care of Marc?" I sure didn't want to do that.

Dr. Foster called me back around midnight. I told him about Marc still bleeding from his trach. I also told him we no longer had a doctor here in Kansas. "Let me make a couple calls out there Christine," Dr. Foster said, "I know a couple of doctors that can work with you." A few minutes later he called me back. "I made you an appointment for nine o'clock in the morning with Dr. LaToye." He told me. I was so grateful. "Everything will be fine," he assured me as we got off the phone.

I sat there at Marc's bedside watching him sleep. I thought, "Why did God save his life to have us go through all of this?" It's not fair; our lives were a living hell! I was doing my best trying to live for God. Everything that could go wrong did. By morning Marcus was back to his normal self. Nothing bothered him. He always had this peaceful look on his face. The bleeding had subsided during the night. I took Marcus that morning to meet our new doctor. He examined him. "Bleeding sometimes results from a lack of humidity. The stint is still in place and everything looks good. Feel free to call me if you have any questions or need anything at all." He said.

The time finally came to go back to Chicago. We were all more than ready to get this stint removed. I couldn't wait to get there! They took Marc into surgery. Jimmie and I paced the floors. I prayed, "Please God, make this happen." It seemed like an eternity before they called us back to talk to the doctor. Dr. Foster came in the room; I could tell by the look on his face it wasn't good news. "I'm sorry, I removed everything. It remained open for about five minutes then collapsed again." He said. I can't tell you the frustration Jimmie and I were feeling. I wanted badly to wake up from this nightmare that seemed to be lasting for years. Dr. Foster went on to say, "I do have another procedure I can try."

Jimmie and Dr. Foster were talking about another surgery when I got up to leave the room.

I was developing an attitude towards God once again. Why wasn't God healing Marc's throat? He healed him of a twisted brain stem, why not his throat? I kept reminding myself of that same ole scripture, "Trust in the Lord with all thine heart, lean not unto thy own understanding." (Proverbs 3:5) This was hard to do; my thoughts kept getting in the way.

Jimmie and I took Marc home with the understanding that Dr. Foster would do another reconstruction at a later date. I was so disappointed. I was learning to pray the Word of God over my situations. I had two children that depended on me. I didn't know how we were going to make it from one day to the next. I had a lot of unanswered questions that made my life difficult. I still had Jimmie to deal with. He was at the point where he couldn't hold a job. His life was a mess. So he wasn't any help to me. I didn't want to live anymore. I knew if it weren't for Marcus I would have checked out long ago.

I was trying to stay active in the church. I wanted to be faithful in my commitment to the Lord. Jimmie and I were sharing a vehicle that was on its last leg. One day it finally broke down. The repairs were going to cost more than the car was worth. Now we have no transportation. I had to depend on people to get me everywhere. To work, church, even to get Marcus to day care. I prayed my prayer of faith. "Dear God, I know that it is your desire that I have dependable transportation, so I ask you for it now. I believe that I receive it, in Jesus name." I began to thank God everyday for my new vehicle. The days turned into weeks; the weeks turned into months. About three months had gone by. After Sunday night service at church a woman approached me with a title to a car. "The Lord told me about three months ago to give this to you; I didn't want to part with it." She said. As she handed me the title to the car I said, "Thank You Jesus!"

God showed himself mightily to me that night. She went on to say, "The car has all new parts on it except the brakes, and you'll need to replace them." I was in heaven, brakes I could handle! I was so happy at that moment, not just for the car, but the fact that God is faithful. He showed me that he really did care about my life.

The months were passing by so quickly. The more I prayed for Jimmie, the more he drank. I quit praying for him. I hated the trach! Every day life was so hard to deal with. I knew God was with me but at times I couldn't feel it. Depression would set in; I'd feel like a failure at every thing I put my hand to. I started going to church less. The next thing I knew I was going out with girls I worked with every chance I got. I started believing a lie. One night I was out at a club I ran into a girl that attended my church. I didn't know her well, other than she was going through a divorce at the time. Her husband and children attended church more than she did. I remembered thinking to myself as we sat there talking, "I'm not doing anything wrong here, just sitting in this club having a few drinks." It wasn't long after that she invited me out again. This was starting to become a habit. This one night a guy came up to our table to say hello to her. He was very good looking. I caught myself staring at him as she introduced us. "Christine, this is my friend Lee," she said as he took my hand. "Would you like to dance Christine?" he said. I didn't hesitate for a moment. I got on my feet and hit the dance floor with this man.

Lee mesmerized me. We spent the rest of that night talking about everything and anything. I told him about my life; he shared his with me. "I was divorced two years ago," he told me. "I have two boys that I don't see very often, my ex-wife and I don't get along very well," he added.

I enjoyed myself so much that night. It was wonderful to have someone to talk to. I liked this guy! I walked into work the next day with Lee on my mind. "Wow Christine, who were you with last night?" one of the girls asked me. Sitting on my station were a dozen of the most beautiful white roses with red tips that I had ever seen. As I removed the card my hands were shaking. I opened it and read, "Beautiful Roses for a Beautiful Lady, Love, Lee." I never received flowers before, what a feeling I had. I was in love!

After a few months of seeing Lee, I agreed to move in with him. Jimmie was upset by the whole arrangement but I didn't care. I moved in with Lee the spring of 1990. I knew at that time I was in trouble. I was living in sin! The conviction I felt was often unbearable. I was happy or at least I thought I was. I was very much in love with Lee. Finally, one day as I was getting ready for work he came in to the bedroom. "Christine, will you be my wife?" he asked as he opened a small box revealing an awesome diamond ring. I couldn't believe it. "Yes," I said. I didn't have to think about it. Lee was a wonderful man! I knew we would be together always. We were best friends!

I felt sorry for Lee at times. I often wondered if he knew what he was getting into. Daniel was a handful now at the age of fourteen. Marcus was a huge responsibility. I knew Lee loved me; we would make it through anything. Lee and I got married in the fall of 1990. I was so excited because now I could go back to church. Isn't it funny how while we are living in sin we stay away from God? All of a sudden I felt worthy enough to go back to him after being away all of this time.

Jimmie met a woman that had three children who lived in his neighborhood. Her name was Jean. Thank You Jesus! He answered my prayers. Jimmie now had someone in his life.

It wasn't long before he hit us with the news that they were moving to Atlanta, Georgia. "Jean's father has a good job for me down there," Jimmie told me. "I can't believe you are going to move so far away," I said. "What about Marcus?" I was raising my voice because I thought once again Jimmie was thinking only of himself. "Let me take him with me Christine!" he responded. "No!" I yelled. "You can't do that, Marcus needs his mother." I added. I was sick from disgust thinking about Jimmie moving away but I knew I had to deal with it. Big Mama always said, "Watch what you pray for, it will happen." I prayed for a long time that Jimmie would meet someone; that he'd get a life of his own. It finally came to pass but for some reason I wasn't as happy about it as I thought I'd be. It was time for Marcus to have another surgery in Chicago. I dreaded going but we knew it had to be done. Jimmie agreed to meet us there. This surgery was very similar to the first one so we knew what to expect this time. However, it didn't make it any easier to get through it. The stint was only in his airway for three months this time rather than six. Lee and I were so broke. We drove up there with Marcus. I wasn't looking forward to the drive back. Lee would have to find us truck stops so we could pull over to put Marcus on his humidifier and suction him. It was a long ride back to Kansas.

We finally arrived back home around six o'clock one night. I was exhausted! When we walked in the door, we discovered that we had no electricity. "Oh God, what are we going to do?" I prayed. Our electricity had been disconnected for non-payment. We had no money till Lee got paid. That wasn't for another two days. I was scared! Marcus had to have humidity and be suctioned. His machines ran off electricity. It was a long night to say the least. We fixed Marcus a bed in the back of the truck. Lee and I took turns driving to the nearest gas station so we could plug Marcs' humidifier in.

God surely looked out for us that night. The next morning Lee was on the phone with every available resource. No one could help us. They either did not do that sort of thing or they had no funds. I finally got some help from the state.

The three months went by so fast! It was time once again to see the streets of Chicago. I hated it there. This time we were only there for a couple of days. Dr Foster came to talk to us after the surgery. "I removed the stint and the airway only stayed open for about five minutes before collapsing again. I'm really sorry." He told us. I could tell that Dr. Foster was frustrated. I was way beyond disappointed. David's words kept ringing in my ears; "He'll not have this trach forever." I've heard many times over, "Our timing is not God's timing." I remember thinking, "How much longer Lord? I'm reaching the end of my rope. I don't know how much more I can handle."

I was very happy being married to Lee, but I felt as though he took on more than he bargained for. We were constantly struggling to pay bills. Lee and I were doing the best we could with what little we had. We all loved going to church. I spent a lot of time with the Lord. I really enjoyed being in his presence. It was my hiding place, where I found strength and joy. I had an inner peace, I couldn't explain it but I knew it was real. There were times however; that something would happen, and then I would withdraw. I'd let days go by without praying or reading my bible. I could never understand why God allowed us to go through so much hell. During this time of our lives I felt as though I were on a roller coaster with God. Up one minute, down the next! There were times that I actually thought I was going to lose my mind! I would get back on my knees in prayer. Somehow I always knew that everything was going to be all right.

LIFE GOES ON

It was time for Marcus to go to kindergarten. He was so excited and so was I. After the last surgery, Marcus now had a voice. It wasn't loud by any means but I could hear him talk. He was ready to go to school. I enrolled him in the public school where we lived. They had a special needs program there for children like Marc. He loved it! I was able to work more hours and it saved me on child care expenses.

The year went by pretty fast with Marcus being in school. Lee and I both were able to work full time jobs however Marcus medical supplies kept us broke. There was never any extra. Utilities kept getting disconnected. Most of the time food was scarce. I hated my life! I thought, "This is all there is to your life Christine, you might as well get used it."

Lee came home from work one day excited to tell me something. "I just found out there is a job opening in a small town south of here for a power plant operator." He said. "I'm going down there tomorrow to apply for this job! It's an increase in pay with better benefits." Lee was excited as he rambled on, "We need to pray about this Christine!" I was excited to say the least; I saw a light at the end of our tunnel! The thought of moving to a new town made me nervous but we decided if Lee got the job it was what God wanted for us. It only took a couple of weeks before we received the news that Lee was hired. I was somewhat nervous about going because I would have to find a new job in this small town. That wasn't going to be easy! All I really knew how to do was cut hair. Lee and I found a place to live in a big old house on a quiet street. We got moved over the Christmas break that year of 1992. "Lee, I think we should check into a private school for Marcus!" I told Lee one night as we were unpacking.

I wasn't happy with the public school and their special needs program. "It's going to be expensive," he said. I agreed with him that for the rest of that year he would go to public school. During the summer we would check in to the private school.

Lee was happy with his job at the city. I had very limited places to apply for work. It was January of 1993 and I desperately needed work. It was cold and snowy out this one afternoon as I wandered in to this restaurant to apply for a waiting table job. "It's better than nothing," I told myself as I walked in the door. I sat down, ordered a cup of coffee and asked for an application. I wasn't sure I wanted to work there, or even if the Lord wanted me there. But I needed a job!

The next thing I knew the manager was sitting across the table from me. His name was Bob. A nice guy; a little high strung. He was very impressed with my application and told me that he would call me. I left there feeling that I could have this job waiting tables if I were persistent. A couple of days went by and I got a call from Bob. "I'd like to set up a time for an interview," he said. We agreed to meet that afternoon. I prayed, "Lord, let me get this job!" I went to the restaurant later that day. Bob and I sat at a booth in the back of the restaurant. "My wife and I are moving to Florida," he said. "I would like to train you to take over my position here as General Manager!" My jaw hit the table. I couldn't believe what I was hearing. I left the restaurant that day on cloud nine. I was starting the following Monday morning. I had no idea what I had gotten myself into. The training wasn't so bad but when Bob left, it was a different story. The staff didn't like me. I worked long days and nights. Lee and I were able to put Marc in the private school. I made good money but I worked hard for it. Marcus was growing up so fast. He was ten years old now.

Daniel was excited about my new job. After I took over the store I would be able to hire him to work in the restaurant. He liked the new town we moved to. It was small but had everything we needed. He never had a hard time making new friends. It wouldn't be long and he would be out of school and starting his own life.

"We've had this trach for seven years!" I told Lee one night as we were discussing another surgery in Chicago. "I hate that trach, I'll never get used to it!" I told him. I hated that thing with a passion. I didn't want to go through another surgery but I knew we were going to have to. I called Jimmie in Atlanta, "Its time once again for a surgery in Chicago," I told him. "I can't take all of this time off from work, could you meet us there and stay with Marc for the last week?" Jimmie agreed.

A couple of weeks later we were back in Chicago. At least it was summer time. We didn't have to fight the cold and snow. We met with Dr. Foster after they got Marcus checked in to the hospital. "I will be doing something a little different this time," he said. "I will be removing the trach and placing the ventilator tube in his airway. I am going to leave it in place for a week." Once again I could hear David's words echo in my mind, "he'll not have this trach for the rest of his life." I have to admit however; I could hardly see Marc without the trach. It had become a part of him.

They took Marc in to surgery the next morning. Lee and I waited in the waiting room. I paced the floor like always. This surgery didn't take near as long as the others. "They have taken Marc in to the intensive care unit," Dr. Foster said as he came walking across the floor. "The surgery went fine; I'll take him back to surgery in seven days to remove the ventilator tube, we'll see how it goes," he added.

I couldn't believe what I saw when I walked in to the intensive care unit. I saw my baby without the trach for the first time in seven years. They had the hole in his throat stitched. The ventilator tube went in through his mouth. Marcus wasn't happy though! "I can't breathe mom," he said with great difficulty. I had to read his lips. The ventilator tube made it hard to understand him, but I knew what he was saying. I kept reassuring him that he could breathe just fine. It was horrible! I sat there looking at him then the thought occurred to me, "Marcus doesn't know life without his trach, he must be petrified!"

The next few days went by so slow. Jimmie was arriving the morning that Dr. Foster was scheduled to remove the ventilator tube. They took Marc back in to surgery. Once again we were in the waiting room. I looked up when I heard Jimmie's voice. "How's Marc doing?" he asked Lee. I just kept looking out the window, wondering what was taking so long. "He's been in there over an hour!" I told Jimmie as I walked over to sit down with him and Lee. "It was supposed to be a simple surgery. I wonder what is taking so long." I said, as I got up to pace the floor again. Dr. Foster finally came to the waiting room. We were anxious to hear the results but I could tell by the look on his face, it wasn't good. "I don't understand," he said. "I'm really sorry but the airway collapsed after a few minutes. I had to put the trach back in." He added, "It's a miracle that Marc has a voice at all, he doesn't have any identifiable vocal cords. They have been damaged beyond repair." I just looked at him, feeling sick to my stomach. Jimmie and Lee talked to Dr. Foster a few minutes more then we went in to see Marc. He wasn't upset; just ready to go home. Lee and I had to get back to work. They were keeping Marc for a few more days. Jimmie agreed to bring him home.

It was a long quiet ride back to Kansas. "These surgeries are so hard on Marc," I told Lee. "I don't want to put him through anymore; I think the next surgery should be Marcus' decision, don't you?" I knew Lee couldn't believe all the pain and heartache we had been through in the past seven years. "I think your right Christine," Lee said, "Dr. Foster said we can always try again when he gets older. He is going to be able to make up his own mind about that." I couldn't get beyond the fact that God hadn't healed Marc's throat. "Why?" I thought. There was a part of me that really did believe; that trach would be gone someday! I learned to be content with the trach. It wasn't as easy for Marc though; he was the one that had to live with it. The children at school would make fun of him and he would come home upset. I always told him, "You are special, don't ever forget that!" Marcus was a great child. He had such compassion, and he was such a giver. He didn't however, have many friends. I tried to make life easier for him but there was only so much I could do.

After Marc arrived home from Chicago, we got on with our lives, as we knew them. I was drifting away from church. My job was difficult! Lee and I started having problems. He finally quit his job for the city. I was the only one working. I was growing to hate my job. I wanted more than ever to quit so that I could concentrate on my family. Dan started dating a girl that worked for me at the restaurant. Her name was Joni. I liked her a lot; she was one of my best workers. Joni and Daniel came to see me at work one day. "Can we talk to you Mom, privately?" he asked me. I was worried because he looked so serious. "Sure," I told him and Joni as we walked back to my office. Dan didn't waste any time as he pulled up a chair next to my desk. "Joni is pregnant Mom." He said. My heart stopped! I didn't know what to do or say. I wanted to scream at him but I knew that wouldn't do any of us any good.

Part of me was excited but another part of me was scared. Dan was barely nineteen and she was sixteen. I decided this pregnancy was something the two of them were going to have to deal with. Lord knows I had enough on my plate at that moment to deal with. Lee and I finally decided it was time to leave that small town. We took Marc and moved into the city with some friends of ours. I hated my life, of course! I didn't see it ever getting any better. The worse thing that I could have done was quit going to church and spending time with the Lord. The things of this world were choking the Word of God that I used to live by. I was tired of being broke. I was tired of the trach. I was also getting more and more tired of Lee. The move to the city would surely be good for us.

I loved being in Kansas City but I hated living with friends. I was able to get a job but Lee didn't. Our friends worked a small home business selling nutritional products. Lee decided he was going to work with them. Alvin and Jenny did okay with their business but Lee wasn't making any money. "I'd like to move into our own place Lee," I told him. I'm tired of being the only one working here! Lee just glared at me, "The business will get better Christine, it takes time." He said. "Marc's school is taking a large portion of my paycheck, we will never be able to move out like this Lee!" I yelled, getting very frustrated with him. "We are not taking Marc out of private school!" I added before he could say anything. Lee stormed out of the room and I sat there wondering, "What happened to this wonderful marriage I used to have?" I could see us drifting apart.

Joni went into labor on December 16 of 1996. We tried to get a hold of Dan; he was working in a nearby town. I went to the hospital to assist Joni. I was so excited seeing our granddaughter come in to this world. Daniel arrived at the hospital shortly after she was born. She was so beautiful and it amazed me at how much she looked like Dan when he was born. They named her Alysan Christine. A few weeks after Aly came I talked to Dan about marrying Joni. "I'm not getting married Mom, not to anyone!" he said. I dropped the subject and decided I would have to pray about this. God would have to change his mind and deal with him on this subject. Dan and I both knew it was a sin to live together out side of marriage. I did it so what more could I expect from my son. Regardless, I had a beautiful little princess! I felt blessed!

Daniel and Joni took the baby and moved to Lawrence, Ks. Lawrence is a college town about twenty-five miles from Kansas City. It wasn't far so we were able to see Aly anytime we wanted to. The months were going by so fast. Marc was getting to be a teenager. I was in his room one day putting away clothes when I came across a notebook that he had been writing in. I was curious about the things he had been writing. I sat down on the edge of his bed and began to read. Then it dawned on me, these were song lyrics!

Lee and Marc came in the door from school that afternoon and I handed the notebook to Marc. "What is all of this Marc?" I asked him as he took the notebook. "These are the lyrics I write Mom, I'm going to be a rapper!" he responded. "Marcus, the music business is a hard business to get involved with. You need to concentrate on school." I told him. He walked out of the room mumbling, "I'm still going to be a rapper!" Lee sat down across from me at the dining room table and asked, "What were the lyrics about?" I was impressed to say the least. "He talks about how God healed him, and how Good the Lord is." I told him. "Really?" Lee asked, rather surprised. Actually I was surprised also, since Marc had to deal with so much from other kids his age. It was plain to see that God had his hand on Marc.

HOMELESS

Things were really bad for Lee and me. We couldn't pay bills. There were so many. Most of them were medical bills that had taken a toll on us. "I think we should file a bankruptcy." I told Lee one night during a heavy discussion about money. We decided to file it because we were so far behind on our car payment. Why did we struggle so hard with our finances? I could believe God for a healing in my own body, I never got sick. If sickness tried to come on me I'd confess the Word concerning healing to receive what I knew God promised me. I walked in divine health. I knew it was mine. But when it came to believing God for a car payment, I struggled. When we were in the church we never tithed. We didn't have the extra money. It took all we had to keep Marc's medical supplies. A surgery would wipe us out for two years. Now, we weren't even going to church anymore. It was hard to pray so I didn't. I got home from work one night and Lee told me, "Alvin and Jenny are selling their house. They are moving back to their home town." They were from a small town in western Kansas. "Its time for us to find a place of our own." Lee said. We were with them for almost two years, how fast the time was going by!

I got a call from my sister Rose in Pennsylvania. We talked from time to time. Our other brothers and sisters didn't have much to do with her either. She had left her husband for another man when I was about twelve years old. They talked bad about her. I knew that mom was living with Rose. "I had to put mom in a nursing home," she said. "I'm not sure how much longer she is going to be with us, I think you should come home to see her." I told Lee, "I really don't want to go but I need to, this may be the last time I see her." Marcus was in Atlanta spending a couple of weeks over the summer with Jimmie.

So I decided to take the trip to see mom. She was in her eighties now. I hadn't seen her in a number of years.

It was June of 1999. I was going to Pennsylvania. At least it was summer! I was going to enjoy this trip. I wanted to see some of my old friends. While I was gone, Lee was going to be looking for a place for us to live. We were out of time. I spent four wonderful days at home. I went to the nursing home to see mom. "I hate it here," she told me. She was in a wheel chair. I could tell it would have been hard for Rose trying to take care of her on her own. I could also tell mom was a little senile. She was repeating herself; talking about strange things. I didn't stay long; I wasn't comfortable there. "I'll be back next year to see you Mom," I told her as I got up to leave. She acted like I wasn't even there. Once again, I was ready to get back home, even though I didn't have one.

Lee came to pick me up at the airport when I returned. On the ride from the airport to Alvin and Jenny's, I could tell something was terribly wrong. Lee was not saying much. I could tell he was preoccupied. We pulled in to the drive way and I got out of the car. Lee got my luggage out of the trunk. I walked in the front door. The house was empty! "Lee, what's going on?" I asked as I walked towards our room. I got to the doorway; our room was empty also. I turned around and saw Lee standing there. I saw two bags of his sitting in the middle of the room. "What is happening here?" I repeated. "I'm leaving Christine, everything is in storage. You can get in there next week to get your things." He couldn't look me in the eye. My heart was beating so hard that it hurt. Lee walked out of the room. He was gone, just like that. No explanation; nothing! Gone! Everything was gone! I stood in the middle of the room; it was spinning. I cried, "God, what happened?" I had nowhere to go, no one to call. Thank God Marcus was at his dads. I didn't know what to do. I had about five dollars cash on me. I got in the car with my bags and headed to the bank.

The account was over drawn. "Oh God, I'm homeless!" At least I had a job, not a good one, but it was a job.

I spent the next couple of weeks sleeping in my car. I called Jimmie, "Please keep Marc there with you till I can get on my feet." He agreed but wasn't happy about it. I knew his wife didn't want Marc there but I couldn't take care of him. I was working at a salon; not making much money. I didn't like it there. A lady that I worked with Joann had invited me to go to her favorite place after work one day for a drink. I agreed to go. They had a deck outside. It was nice out there. I didn't tell the people I worked with any of my business. I was a private person with too much pride. Joann and I were in conversation about work when this gentleman walked over to our table. "Can I buy you ladies a drink?" he asked staring right at me. Joann responded, "Sure, have a seat." I felt a little uncomfortable but he seemed okay.

We sat there for what seemed like hours talking about work and money. "I own a home remodeling company," he said. "Would you be interested in doing some part time work for me?" I listened as he continued, "I pay cash! He went on to say that he had a few guys that worked for him and that he would be happy to train me. "Was God answering a prayer?" I thought. His name was Tim; he had a home remodeling company. He wanted to hire me! He was going to pay me twelve dollars an hour, cash money. This sounded too good to be true. Tim gave me his number "Call me if you're interested." He said as he got up to leave. "You should do it," Joann told me as we were leaving the deck that day. She was going home. I was going to find some place to park my car for sleep that night. Daniel and Joni had issues of their own without me adding to it so I couldn't go there. Joni was pregnant again. Dan wasn't happy about it. He wasn't even staying there with her most of the time. I felt bad for Aly, not having her Mom and Dad together.

I went to a service station and cleaned myself up before my long night ahead of me. I couldn't help thinking about working for this man. Before I knew it I had talked myself into it. I lay in the front seat of my car that night thinking about Lee. I cried so hard. I didn't know what was going to become of Marcus or me for that matter. I knew he couldn't stay at his dad's for too long. Jimmie and his wife did not want Marc down there in Atlanta. I missed him so much. I worried about him constantly.

I called Tim the next morning. "I want the job." I told him. "That's great Christine!" he exclaimed. "Meet me on the deck this afternoon about four o'clock to discuss it further." I was so excited, hoping I could make enough money to get a place to live so I could get Marc back home with me where he belonged. I met with Tim later that day. I found out right away that he liked to drink, a lot! We sat outside on the deck. It was extremely hot! The cold beer we were drinking went down so easy. I left that place after dark and realized that I was drunk. I had to drive from there. I got in to the car and started driving. I headed out of the city. Of course the alcohol made me feel even more depressed than I already was. I was determined that night to end my life. I didn't like where it had ended up. I tried to run my car off the road a few times but I couldn't do it. Something kept telling me, "What about Marcus?" I knew his dad didn't want him. I was all that he had. I was hurting so badly down inside. The pain was all too familiar. I knew I had to get a grip on things. I pulled on to a dirt road to sleep that night with hopes of a better day tomorrow. I was starting a new job!

The next morning I showed up at the address that Tim gave me the night before. I met a young man that I was going to be working with. His name was Donny. He was a nice kid about nineteen years old.

We were working on a big house, prepping it for an exterior paint job. I was scrapping off old paint and priming bare wood. It was fun, but so very hot outside in the sun. I didn't see Tim much that day but he did come by to take us to lunch. I was starving and had no money. It was like he read my mind, "Here is twenty dollars to get you through the week," he said handing the bill to me. "Oh, thank you!" I said taking it from him. Tim never asked where I lived. I didn't volunteer any information. I just couldn't wait to get paid. I found out Tim lived in a big house with some of his friends. "After work we will go get cleaned up at my place and go for drinks." He told me. I said, "sure, its sounds good to me." I was thinking about a shower, how nice a shower was going to be. Tim and I got cleaned up, and then went to the deck for drinks again. He was so much fun and we met some of his friends there. It wasn't long before I was enjoying myself. I was also drinking more than I ever had in my life. The drinking made it easier for me to get on with things. I didn't have to think about my situation at the moment plus the fact that Marcus was in Atlanta.

I called Marcus every other day. Every time Tim gave me some money I would send it down to Jimmie to help take care of Marc. "Mom, I want to stay down here," Marcus told me on the phone one day. I was almost ready to move in to my own apartment. "Marcus, please, you need to come home." I pleaded. "It will be ok mom, I will come home for Christmas." He assured me. I told Jimmie he needed to put Marc in private school but he said there weren't any in his area. "He will be fine in our school here Christine." Jimmie said. I missed Marc so much that drinking was the only way I could handle him being gone.

Over the next few weeks, I started telling Tim about my life. We got to be good friends. Once he found out I was living in my car he helped me find an apartment.

I had managed to save enough for the deposit and rent. Since Marc was in Atlanta I only needed a one bedroom for now. Tim and I were getting to be good friends. I liked hanging out with him. He was very good to me. I look back now realizing if it hadn't have been for Tim, I don't know what would have become of us.

I put God on a shelf for the next year like I thought he had done with me the past couple of years. I missed my life with the Lord but spending time with Tim and drinking all of the time, I was able to put him out of my mind. I was having the time of my life. I got moved into my apartment. It was so nice. I didn't have much so I had to buy everything. When Lee left he took almost everything we had. Tim would take me shopping at the mall. He would buy me nice things. I wasn't used to any of this. We went to the finest restaurants to eat and shopped at the best stores. I loved it! I would go see Joni and Aly from time to time. We didn't see much of Daniel. I was excited for Aly's second birthday. The new baby was due at Christmas time that year. Joni and I planned Aly's birthday party and Dan was going to be there. Dan called the morning of Aly's birthday party. "Mom, Joni is at the hospital, she is in labor." He said. "I'm on my way," I told him getting off the phone. By the time I arrived at the hospital Conner Jack was born. He was so precious. He looked a lot like Dan. Aly and Conner, born on the same day, two years apart!

It was Christmas time. Marc was coming home. He was sixteen now. I hadn't seen Marc since I sent him to his dad's. I was so excited to see him when I picked him up at the airport. "Marcus, you've gotten so tall, I've missed you so much," I said as I hugged and kissed him. We got in the car and he proceeded to tell me all about Atlanta. "Jean left dad, I know it's because I'm there," he told me. I knew I would hear about it from Jimmie. It would be my fault.

"I met a lady that lives down the street from us," he went on. "She has a music studio mom; she is going to help me do an album." I suddenly knew that was why Marc wanted to be there. I would have him with me for the next three weeks! I would try to convince him to stay.

We had a really nice Christmas. I didn't drink much while Marc was home, other than an occasional glass of wine. One night I was awakened by a noise in the living room. I got up, knowing that Marc was asleep on the sofa. I couldn't believe what I saw. Marcus was on the floor, on his hands and knees. I walked over to him, "Marcus, are you all right?" I said. At that moment he fell over on to his back. Fear swept over me. "Marcus," I said as I reached to help him to his feet. He was soaked from his waist down. "What's wrong with you?" I cried. He was so heavy I couldn't lift him. I picked up the phone to call Tim. "I need you to come over right away, something is wrong with Marc," I said frantically. "What's wrong?" Tim asked me. "I don't know, he seems delirious, totally out of it," I exclaimed, "Please hurry!" Tim responded, "I'm on my way, you better call an ambulance." I got off the phone with Tim and called for an ambulance. Tim only lived a few blocks away so he was at my door in a matter of minutes. I kept trying to talk to Marc. "Someone must have given him something," I told Tim. "Marc is a good kid, why would someone want to hurt him?" Tim just looked at me as we heard the knock on the door. The ambulance was finally here. The ambulance attendant asked me all kinds of questions about Marc. "Does he do drugs? What about alcohol?" He asked. "No!" I yelled. "Something is terribly wrong here, please help him!" I pleaded. Tim and the ambulance attendant were trying to get Marc to his feet to no avail. They couldn't keep him up so they had to put him on a stretcher. Tim agreed to drive me to the hospital.

I stood by Marcus' hospital bed once again. "Please God, let him be okay." I prayed. The nurses started running all kinds of tests on him. I paced the floor as Tim kept reassuring me that everything was going to be okay. A nurse finally came in as Marc was starting to come around. She quickly reached for a pan as he was starting to vomit. "His alcohol blood level is very high," she told us. "This looks like wine or something that he is throwing up here." I was in shock! Not Marcus! She went on to say, "He's going to be fine! We will watch him for the next few hours." I couldn't believe what I was hearing. "Marcus got drunk Christine," I heard Tim say as I remembered the wine that was sitting on my kitchen counter. "Oh God," I thought, "Marcus got in to my wine!"

After a few hours Tim and I took Marc home. I kept thinking, "Why would Marc do this? He knew better than this." Not even accepting that fact that I was doing it also. What more could I expect from him? Marc was leaving in a couple of days. I didn't want to spend the time we had left fighting over this incident. Marc assured me that he knew it was wrong and that he wouldn't do it again. I put Marc on a plane back to his dad's in Atlanta. School would be out in five months. I hoped then to convince Marc to stay with me. I called Jimmie to talk to him about Marcus' drinking episode. "I think its time for him to get counseling," I told him. "I can't afford that Christine; you'll have to pay for it!" He said. I agreed. I also told Jimmie he needed to get Marc on disability. I knew they went by our income but with Marc being with his dad I thought he would qualify. Jimmie started working on it. He informed me that Marc could get it as soon as he turned eighteen. I knew with the disability his medical expenses would be covered.

I called Atlanta at least once a week to talk to Marc. "Is everything okay there?" I would ask. "I'm fine, but I hate this school Mom," Marc would tell me. Then he would get off that subject to talk about the lady with the recording studio. I could hear the excitement in his voice. I was hoping that this lady would not disappoint him. "I've written a lot of songs for my first album. She says I have talent!" he would tell me. I knew he did! I hoped more than anything he would make it.

It was time to get a divorce from Lee. I had not seen or heard from him in a long time. "I know a good lawyer that won't charge you much for your divorce Christine." Tim told me one night. I was anxious to get it over with. I knew where Lee was working. That was the only address I had for him. Tim introduced me to Scott Pearson. Mr. Pearson took my information and told me he would mail Lee the papers to sign. "If Lee does not contest the divorce you won't need to be in court." He told me. I remember thinking as I left his office, "Ten years of marriage! How is it dissolved so easily?" I felt so empty, so hurt! I couldn't help thinking about Lee the rest of that afternoon. Where was he? How was he feeling about all of this? I had a feeling I would never know the answers. I got the news that Big Mama died the first week in May of 2000. "She had a stroke Christine, and died shortly after." Jimmie told me. "We have to go to Louisiana for Mama's funeral," I couldn't believe Big Mama was gone. Oh how I would miss that woman! Marcus didn't know Big Mama very well. I loved her; she was a wonderful woman! I knew that she was with the Lord! Jimmie and Marc went to Louisiana for Mama's funeral. I prepared for Marc's homecoming the first of June. I was overwhelmed to say the least. Marc had a drinking problem that Jimmie informed me was getting worse. Then the news that Big Mama was gone!

I couldn't believe how time was going by so quickly. I kept working with Tim. I really enjoyed my work. Tim wanted me to go to the deck for a party one night. I agreed to go. I couldn't believe there were so many people there. The first Wednesday of May was the opening of the deck party for the summer. I was sitting there at this little bar beside Tim when I looked up to see a man walking through the crowd of people. Our eyes met. I smiled at him thinking, "Nice looking man!" A few minutes later I saw him again only this time he was the one smiling. I returned his smile as he disappeared in to the crowd. Not long after that I felt a tap on my shoulder. I turned around surprised to see that man standing there behind a woman. "My name is Lori, this is my brother Kevin," she said with a grin on her face. "He wanted to meet you but he wasn't sure if you were alone or with that guy sitting next to you." I immediately responded, "I'm here with friends!" Kevin heard my response as I stretched my hand out to him. "How are you doing?" he said with this deep voice. I smiled at him; very impressed with this man. I'm on my way out but I'd like to get your number and call you sometime." He said as I was fumbling to get a pen out of my bag. We exchanged numbers and he left as fast as he showed up!

Kevin was still on my mind when I got home that night. "I wonder if he will call," I kept thinking. The next day was one of the longest days. I couldn't wait to get home. I ran in the door; straight for my phone to check messages. I was so disappointed! I really wanted this guy to call. Later that evening the call came. I picked up the phone and heard this deep voice, "Christine?" I was so excited my words got stuck in my throat. "How are you doing?" he said as I was gathering my thoughts about what to say to this man. "I'm doing good, thanks!" I responded. "Tomorrow night I am meeting my brother and sister for some dinner and some live blues music! I was wondering if you would like to come along?" he said.

I wanted to go badly but I didn't want to sound too anxious. "I'd like that," I said. He gave me directions to the restaurant. We agreed to meet there. I could tell he wasn't much of a phone person because that was the extent of our conversation. I didn't care! I wanted to know more about this man.

It was a Friday night! I finally had a date I was looking forward to! I arrived at the restaurant and met his family. I was having a nice time but Kevin seemed preoccupied. "We have to go!" I heard him say to his brother and sister. I wasn't ready to go, but I didn't have a choice. Kevin stood up and pulled out my chair. We said our goodbyes and headed to the parking lot. "Thanks for coming Christine," he said as he opened my car door. He gave me a little kiss, "I will call you!" he said. I got into my car. He was out of site by the time I got my key into the ignition. "He sure had some place to be in a hurry," I thought. "Maybe he will call me tomorrow. If he doesn't, oh well, so much for that!" The next day was Saturday. I didn't do much. I stayed close to my apartment hoping that Kevin would call. He didn't! Sunday morning however, Kevin called to see if I'd like to go for a ride with him down to the river market. I was excited once again! I really wanted to know more about this man. I was attracted to him in a strange way. There was something about him.

Kevin picked me up around noon that day. It was a beautiful, warm, sunny May afternoon. He was driving a mustang convertible with the top down. "Have you ever been married Kevin," I asked him as we were just getting on the highway headed for downtown. "No, never have been married," he said smiling at me. "I've never had any children, but I do have a dog!" he added. "Oh no, I don't like dogs," I thought. Kevin went on, "His name is Louie! On our way back I will take you by my house so you can meet him."

I smiled at him as I thought, "I don't want to meet this dog!" Kevin and I had a wonderful afternoon at the river market getting to know one another. It went by too fast. I kept thinking, "This man is too good to be true! No ex-wives to deal with. No children. I loved children but after raising Marc; I didn't want to deal with another child.

It wasn't long after that first date; Kevin and I were spending most of our free time together. He worked as a mechanic at a shop near his home. When he got off work he would go home to feed Louie then come to see me. I would have his dinner waiting when he walked in my door. I knew before long; I was falling in love with this man. Kevin was different than other men I met. There was a quiet side to him that bothered me however. Like he had another life going on that I didn't know about.

After dinner one night, Kevin and I settled down on the sofa to talk. "I have something I need to tell you Christine!" he said. I just looked at him afraid of what was coming. It was too late for this man to give me devastating news; I was in love! "I have a cocaine habit, I've been doing cocaine for about fifteen years," he said with his eyes looking at the floor. "Oh God, what do I do now?" I thought. "I love you Christine, I'm not going to lose you because of this!" he went on trying to reassure me he was giving it up. "I will not have this in my life Kevin," I told him. I was heart broken! I had to prepare myself for what was going to happen between Kevin and me. He would either give it up, or I would give him up!

SELF ABUSE

Marcus came home in June. Kevin and I had been dating for a month now. Marcus had changed so much in the past few months. Jimmie and I could hardly talk on the phone without ending up in an argument about Marc. I was determined to have a great summer with the guys. They got along great. "Marc, why don't you stay here with me and go to school here this year?" I asked him one afternoon. "I can't do that mom; I have things going on in Georgia." He said. I didn't argue with him. "Does your dad have you in counseling?" I asked. I knew I was sending more than enough money down there each week. "Dad took me a couple of times but he doesn't have the money for counseling, I'll be all right," He assured me.

The end of June I got a call from my sister Rose. "Mom is in the hospital, she is not responding much. You better come home. The doctor doesn't give her much time." She said. I didn't want to go once again. Mom was now eighty-five years old so I felt I had to go. Kevin agreed to keep an eye on Marc for me. The first day of July, I was on a flight to Pennsylvania. During the flight, I reflected back on my childhood with my mother. "She failed me as a mother," I thought, "but I also failed her as a daughter. I have to let all of this bitterness go for once and for all." I remembered thinking, "My father died without knowing how much I loved him, I'll not let my mother go this way also."

I walked in to the hospital room where I knew Rose would be waiting for me. She greeted me and said, "Mom's not doing well, I told her you were coming." She added, "The doctor says he believes she can hear us when we talk to her."

I looked around the room; one of my brothers was sitting in a chair up against the wall at the feet of the hospital bed. Standing around my mom were the other four sisters. It was like they were guarding her from me. I couldn't bear being in the room. Nothing had changed after all of these years. They still acted like I had never been born. "I have to get out of here Rose," I told her as I was heading towards the door. "I'm tired; it's been a long day. I'm not in the mood for this." I said hugging her. "I'll be back tomorrow." I left the hospital room feeling the knives they were throwing in my back. I just wanted to see my mother for five minutes.

The next morning Rose and I went to the hospital. Everyone was there; mom was doing about the same. "Can we all leave so Christine can have a few minutes alone with mom?" Rose said to my sister's. They hesitated as they all walked around the bed to leave. "Thank You Lord!" I said to myself as I watched them go. I walked over to the bed looking at my mom's lifeless body lying there. I didn't remember her ever looking so old. She was hooked up to an IV along with a feeding tube. How familiar the scene was to me. "Mom, it's me," I said as tears were starting to burn my eyes. "I don't have much time, but I want you to know how much I love you! I have been a horrible daughter. I hope you forgive me for all the pain I caused you. You're my mother; nothing else matters." I saw a few tears run down her face. I could sense that she was hearing everything I was saying to her. "I'm leaving tomorrow morning to go back to Kansas. I won't be back. I knew as I was sitting there that the Lord was taking her to be with him. I said goodbye to my mom that day with the full assurance that we had settled our differences. I got up from her bedside knowing that I would never see her again as I walked out of the room. The next morning I arrived back in Kansas and got the call from Rose that mom had died that night.

I enjoyed the rest of the summer with Marc before he went back to his dad's. Kevin and I spent all of our free time together. Joni would bring Aly and Conner to Kansas City from time to time. Oh how I loved those babies. Daniel and Joni were still not together so I didn't see him very often. "I'd like to have a birthday party for Aly and Conner in December Christine." Joni told me one afternoon as I sat there looking at my grandchildren playing in the yard. They were growing up so fast. I assured her, "I wouldn't miss it for anything." Aly was going to be four years old and Conner would be two. I was disappointed in Dan for not being with his children, but I couldn't say anything. He was never around his father.

My lease was up in November that year on my apartment. "Why don't you let the apartment go Christine? You can move in with me!" Kevin said. I wanted to but the conviction I felt was overwhelming. When we are away from God, he is still speaking to our hearts. Here I am, thinking about marriage again. I felt like the woman at the well. (John 4:18) I was in love with this man. I wanted to be his wife. I told Kevin about my past failures living for God so he knew how I felt about the situation. I agreed to move in with him. About two weeks past when Kevin came home one night with a beautiful ring! "I want you to be my wife Christine!" he said. I was so excited, "Yes Kevin, I want to be your wife." Not long after that we set a wedding date of May 26, 2001.

It was Christmas time once again and Marcus was coming home. I went to pick him up at the airport. "Look at you, so grown up!" I exclaimed. We hugged as we headed for the door. "What happened to your face Marc?" I asked him noticing that he had some black and blue areas on his cheek and around his eyes. "I got into a fight with a guy at school mom; it's not a big deal." He told me. I could tell he didn't want to talk about it so I dropped it.

We talked on the ride home about the wedding. "We've decided to get married in Jamaica, Marc!" I said. He looked over at me and said, "For real?" I laughed, "Yes, for real!" I was so happy that I was scared. In my life, the moment I was happy something devastating was about to happen. That was one thing I could count on! For now, I had Kevin, and Marc was home for Christmas! I felt I had a future. Kevin would trip up once in a while with the cocaine but I knew he was trying. He would be totally clean by the time we were married or there would be no wedding.

After Christmas it was time for Marc to go back to his dad's. I was in the kitchen one morning and Marc walked in. "How are you this morning Marcus?" I asked him as he walked towards the refrigerator. "I'm okay," he said. I looked over at him. I was shocked at what I saw! His face was swollen and his right eye was bruised. "Marcus, what happened to you?" My heart stopped, I knew immediately that he had done this to himself! I felt sick to my stomach! I didn't know what to do. I felt hopeless! "What would inspire him to do this?" I thought. "I don't want to talk about it!" Marc yelled as he stormed out of the kitchen.

I called Jimmie that morning. "Marcus got up this morning with his face all beat up!" I yelled. "He is doing this to himself! What is going on down there?" I hardly gave Jimmie time to get a word in, I was so angry! "I thought he might be doing something like that Christine, I saw him with a couple black eyes last month. He told me he got in to a fight so I left it alone." I didn't know what to say to him, "Jimmie, you have to put him in counseling, this is not normal!" I said. I got off the phone with Jimmie under the assumption that he would get him into counseling immediately. Marc and I didn't talk about the incident again. It was time for him to go back to Georgia so I took him back to the airport.

"You don't have to go Marc, you can stay here!" I told him as he was checking in at the airline. "I'll be all right mom." He said. I was so tired of hearing that from him.

For the next couple of weeks, I couldn't concentrate on anything. My mind was fixed on Marcus. "Why was he doing this? Is his pain that deep?" I kept thinking. It wasn't more than a week later that Jimmie called. "I'm sending him back to you! I can't do anything with him! He is down here drinking and doing drugs. He won't go to school most of the time, I can't deal with this anymore Christine!" Jimmie yelled hysterically. "Fine," I told him, "send him home!" A few days later I picked Marc up at the airport, so relieved to have him back with me. I knew I was going to have to undo all the damage done to him while he was in Atlanta, but I was confident that I could handle it.

The first thing I did was get Marc enrolled in school. It was a public school but one for special needs children. Children that had trouble with the law, or emotionally challenged that didn't fit in to the normal high school scene. I then got him a counselor at our local mental health facility. Things went really well in the beginning. Kevin was stressed; he got more than he bargained for. He wasn't quite sure how to deal with Marc, but neither was I! This was new to me. I wanted to reach out to God. I needed his help now more than ever before. I was living in sin so asking God for help right now was out of the question.

Marcus was getting counseling once a week. He was so hateful; I didn't like to go in there with him. His attitude was horrible! He didn't care about anything. His language made my skin crawl. One day we did talk about his self-abuse. "Marcus, your face is so beautiful, look at what you are doing to it!" I told him.

"I'm not going to do it any more mom," he said. It sounded good but I wasn't sure he meant it. I convinced myself that the counseling would eventually pull him out of what ever it was that he was going through.

I started getting calls from the school. “We need to set up an appointment with you concerning Marcus’ behavior.” The school psychologist told me. He was being rebellious and not participating in anything. I was getting really worried! “Marcus, I don’t know what to do for you; how to help you.” I told him one afternoon when I picked him up from school. I saw some cuts on his left forearm. It nauseated me! “You can’t do this Marcus, if you continue I’m going to have you hospitalized.” I told him. I noticed that he wasn’t cutting very deep, just enough to make him bleed. You can’t even imagine how it makes a mother feel to know that her child is in so much pain emotionally that they would abuse themselves, unless you’ve experienced it. I called Marc’s counselor for help! She agreed to meet with me. “Marc is inflicting pain on himself because he has a hard time dealing with his emotions,” she told me. “He gets overwhelmed and frustrated! He then takes it out on himself.” She added. “I can’t deal with this!” I told her. I was screaming on the inside. I was angry and didn’t want to hear what she was saying. “Just be patient with him while we work out these issues in his life.” She said as I got up to leave. This was something I never dreamed that I would go through; the sad thing was that I didn’t know how.

A few days after I met with the counselor the school called me once again. “We can’t find Marcus,” the principle told me. “He stormed out the door. We watched him walk around the property. I went out to talk him into coming back inside. He agreed to come back. I gave him a few minutes to get back in here but he disappeared. We can’t find him anywhere.” As I drove over to the school I couldn’t help thinking, “Dear God, what do I do with this boy?”

I pulled up to the school and ran in the front door. The principle met me in the hallway. “We found him Christine; he was in one of the boys bathrooms. He was hiding back in a corner in a fetal position, crying!” This mans words tore me up inside. I cried so hard, I stood there with my face in my hands sobbing. I could feel Marcus' pain again.

I got Marc home that afternoon with the intention of forcing him to talk to me. "Mom, you don't understand!" he yelled. "Understand what Marc? I want to understand so that I can help you!" I said. "You need to talk to me, tell me what is going on in your head." As Marc sat there across from me at the kitchen table that afternoon I knew something was terribly wrong. I was in denial! I had been in denial all this time. I didn't want to accept that fact that Marcus had serious emotional issues. I was ready to listen to him! I wanted us to confront these issues! "A lot of bad things happened to me in Georgia, mom." He told me. "What things?" I said feeling sicker to my stomach than ever before. Afraid of what I would hear. It was like he knew what I was thinking because at that moment he looked at me and said, "I can't tell you, I don't want to talk about it! I will be okay!" I shook my head; I wanted to confide in Kevin. He saw some of the things going on with Marc, but I didn't reveal much to him. I didn't want to burden Kevin with all of this. We were getting married in a couple of months. "If only I could take this to the Lord," I thought. "God could fix this horrible mess!" In my mind I kept hearing, "You're living in sin Christine, you are on your own!"

The first week in April was another bad chapter in my book of life. Marcus was out of control! One night he had cut on his arms so bad I knew he would be scarred for life. Kevin and I couldn't take anymore. We took him to a local hospital. They admitted him to the sixth floor psychiatric ward. I wanted to die! The staff told me they would keep him for up to a week. During that time they would get him on medications to help him while they did evaluations. Kevin and I went to visit him every night. It was a horrible scene. Marcus was so drugged that I couldn't even talk to him. On day six, I requested to take him home with me against the doctor's recommendations. The doctor wanted to send him to another hospital for further evaluations. "Absolutely not!" I said as I signed Marc's release. "I'm taking him home."

Kevin and I sat in the waiting room for Marcus. "Are you sure you know what your doing Christine?" Kevin said shaking his head at me. "No Kevin, I don't! All I do know is that no one is going to institutionalize my son!" I kept thinking, "What if something is terribly wrong with Marc? What if I can't help him? What if he seriously hurts himself or someone else?" Kevin and I took Marcus home that Friday evening. The next few weeks went by fast! Kevin and I were planning our wedding at the end of May. Marc and I kept seeing the counselor. I was learning a lot about how to deal with head injury people. It took patience; lots of patience dealing with Marcus.

Kevin and I stayed positive with him. Medication was helping him sleep at night so the cutting wasn't nearly as frequent as it was in the past. "Christine, Marcus will be eighteen this summer!" Kevin told me as the three of us sat down to dinner one night. I knew something was coming I didn't really want to hear. "I'm going to teach Marc how to drive so he can get his license!" he added. I nearly chocked on my food! "Are you sure about this?" I asked. Marcus spoke up, "Mom, I can do this!" I looked at Kevin while Marc was pleading his case. Kevin interrupted, "I'll take him down to get him a permit. Then I'll let him start driving. If he can pass the driving test, then he is entitled to a driver's license!" "Okay!" I said hesitantly.

The day finally came when Marc said, "Mom, Kevin is taking me to take my driving test tomorrow, sure hope I pass it! I know I will pass the driving part, but I'm not sure about the written test." I was so hoping that he did. He needed some confidence in himself. He passed the driving part but did have to take the written over again. "What an accomplishment Marc!" I told him as he came running in the house to show me his driver's license. I was so proud of him.

DRUGS AND ALCOHOL

I never thought the end of May would ever get here. Kevin and I had an awesome wedding. A few days after we were married we moved into our new home. For the first time in my life I had my own home. I loved it! "Lord, I know I'm not living for you, but I feel so blessed right now," I thought as I was sitting outside on the front steps. "Marcus is doing much better; I have a wonderful new husband, and a new home! Thank you Jesus, because I believe that every good thing does come from you!"

"There is an organization that works with head injury people that I'd like to put you in touch with Christine." Marc's counselor told me at one of our sessions. "They will work with Marc in dealing with issues. They will also help him with basic living skills. Marc turns eighteen soon! He will qualify for disability which will provide the funding." I was so excited. I could see a light at the end of the tunnel. I turned in all of the necessary paperwork. Marcus was approved for a Head Injury waiver provided by the state.

I was still very concerned about Marc. Kevin would get so angry with him for getting into his liquor. I knew Marc was doing drugs as well. He started meeting guys but I knew they weren't his friends. He was getting drugs from them. I couldn't wait for him to turn eighteen to get started with the community service program. Marcus also had a bad attitude where females were concerned. I could only imagine because he was at the age where girls would normally be a big part of a young man's life. Marc had to deal with his trach along with his other issues. "There are no good females in the world mom," he told me one night. "They all sleep around with every body!"

I couldn't believe the things he was saying. "Marcus!" I yelled, "Don't judge all females by what you know about a few of them! There are a lot of nice girls out there!" He wouldn't listen to me. Every time he met a girl she would make him mad. Kevin and I would end up with holes in our walls or the doors kicked in. It was a lot to deal with. I found myself drinking more and more just to get up in the morning to deal with another day with this boy!

The time finally came for the community service to work with Marc. He was assigned a worker that spent a few hours a week with him. He also had a case manager that monitored the worker. Unfortunately, the workers were usually females. "I don't know what is going on," I told Kevin one night. "Marcus is running these workers off." They would get him a worker; she would be with us for a couple weeks then she would be gone. Marc would go with out a worker till they could get another one. Months went by! Things were getting worse instead of better. Kevin and Marc were at one another's throat constantly.

Marc and I got into an argument one day about his counselor. He didn't want to see her anymore. I called her with the news. "I don't know what to do about the drugs and alcohol he is using," I told her. "Most of the time head injury people will self medicate," she said. "Try to get him into a substance abuse program." I told her I would but really didn't see Marcus going. I knew life was difficult for him. To be honest I don't know how he made it through any given day. We were not living for the Lord. I was all that Marcus had. Every one he came in to contact with used and abused him. He was so hungry for acceptance from anyone it made him very vulnerable. "I have to protect him Kevin," I said in a heated discussion we were having one night. "Everything Marc is feeling, everything he is going through, he doesn't deserve this. I wish I could take it all away from him, but I don't know how!"

Marcus would tell me, "Mom, I don't think like other people think!" I knew he didn't! I was doing all I could just being there for him.

"I found Marcus a car Christine," Kevin told me one afternoon. "I think he needs more responsibilities, he may start to grow up." I cringed, "I'm not sure that's a good idea right now!" I knew he was going to do it anyway. Marcus was so excited! It really was a nice car. He was so proud of it! Marc had a couple of friends that came around quite often. I worried about him being gone with them because I knew they got high all the time. Marc was drinking a lot. "Don't drink and drive your car Marcus!" I told him one afternoon. "That's asking for trouble." He would get so mad at me!

Sure enough, one night a police officer brought him home. I opened the door to see Marcus standing there wobbling as the officer was reading off the charges. "Marcus wrecked his car, it's been impounded!" the officer said. I just looked at Marcus, disgusted with what I was hearing. "Go upstairs to bed Marc!" I said as he walked by me to the stairs. "He is very intoxicated; he drove his car in to a yard. The airbag went off so it was a hard impact." The officer added. I noticed Marc's face banged up, realizing now that it must have been caused by the airbag. I must say that I was surprised that the police brought Marc home but I was glad they did.

The next morning wasn't a good one. "We buy you a car; you drive drunk and wreck it!" Kevin screamed at Marc. I looked at Marc shaking my head. His face was black and blue with a small cut under his right eye. It was badly swollen. "We have to go get this car out of tow, they charge by the day." Kevin went on. So we all went out to look at the damage done to his car. It was ugly but it was still drivable. I read the officers report of what Marc was charged with. "I need to hire Marc an attorney Kevin. He is being charged with a DUI."

I still had Scott Pearson's phone number in my address book. I had not talked to him since he filed my divorce for me from Lee. "Mr. Pearson is no longer with our office," the secretary told me. "I can put you through to Clint Hamilton." She went on. "He schedules his own appointments!" I agreed to talk to him. We set up an appointment for the next day. I liked Mr. Hamilton. I gave him the police report that the officer gave me. "I will call you in a couple of days." He said as I left his office. I was shocked when he called saying, "I got Marc off that DUI!" Somehow, when Marc wrecked his car he walked away from the accident. He walked a few blocks, ending up in another town. He was then arrested by the wrong police making it some sort of technicality. I was happy about it but I still knew that this was just the beginning of what was yet to come.

A couple of months went by before Marcus was talking about buying another car. "I hope you've learned your lesson Marc, about drinking and driving!" Kevin told him. We both knew that we couldn't keep him from doing anything he wanted to do. He was an adult and made sure we knew it. Before long, Marc had another vehicle. I had a feeling it wouldn't last long. It didn't! The police pulled him over a few doors down from where we live. They arrested him and took him to jail this time. I went up to the police station to pick him up. The officer releasing him to me said, "Marcus got a citation for a hit and run! He hit a car that was stalled out on a main street. The caller described your son and the car he was driving. Another officer spotted your son driving as the call came in and followed him to your street. Marcus also got a citation for a DUI; he is under the influence right now." I grabbed Marc by the arm as I led him towards the door. "Your driving days are over!" I yelled. He replied with,

“Whatever!” I wanted to slap him silly but I knew that talking to him now was a waste of time.

I had to call Clint again! I was embarrassed to say the least. Kevin and I finally got Marc to realize he was not ready for the responsibility of driving. The community service had not been working with Marc for a long time now so I wasn’t sure what to do with this kid. I would call them from time to time. “We have a shortage of workers right now. As soon as we find one for Marcus we will let you know.” They would tell me. Kevin and I just took each day as it was handed to us. We were as bad as Marc at that time. I was drinking quite a lot. It had become an everyday occurrence for me. I knew that I had to do something with Marc or our lives were going to be over. He was stealing from us, every chance he could get. I couldn’t leave any liquor or money lying around. Kevin and Marc would get into horrible fights that ended up with things broken. “I feel so bad for him Christine, but what are we supposed to do? He has no respect for anything or anybody!” Kevin said. “I don’t know Kevin, I just don’t want to give up on him. I don’t want to just throw him away!” I told him. “He’s got to go Christine!” Kevin said. I knew he was right, but I didn’t know how to do it.

I had reached the end of my rope. Marcus was a mess! Talking to him about counseling or anything like it was out of the question. “Marcus, we are going to find you an apartment, you need to move out and be on your own.” I told him. I could tell he wasn’t excited about it but it had to be done. I found Marc an apartment within minutes of our house. I thought it would be okay because I knew I would see him everyday. Kevin and I got Marc moved in to his new apartment in November of 2002. I made sure he had everything he needed. I kept hoping that the community service would find a good qualified person to work with Marcus. His case manager introduced us to a young lady who was going to step in as a worker for Marcus but at this time we didn’t see much of her.

In December our lives changed forever! It was a bad week to start with. Marcus was very depressed; I could feel it. His community service worker called him to tell him that she would be able to spend some time with him that week. She never did call or show up. I called Marc on a Thursday afternoon; I could hear such disappointment in his voice. "Mom, there is nothing to do, I hate it here," he told me. "Marc, as soon as the community service can find someone to work with you, they will help you find a job. You will be able to start working on your high school diploma." I said. I was trying desperately to give him hope, something to look forward to.

I got home from work later that evening. The phone rang the moment I walked in the door. "Mom," I heard as I barely got hello out of my mouth! "Will you come get me?" I hesitated for a moment. "Marcus, I'm so tired tonight, I'll come over first thing in the morning to get you." I said. "We can spend the day together." He got quiet for a moment; I knew he was thinking of a way to convince me I needed to come get him. "I feel like something bad is going to happen to me tonight Mom!" he said. We talked for a while as I kept trying to reassure him everything was going to be fine. I got off the phone with an uneasy feeling in the pit of my stomach. "You can't go running over there every time he calls Christine," Kevin told me. "I feel so bad for him Kevin, he doesn't know how to deal with the feelings he is having!" I said. "I know I have to let him grow up, but I don't want him to get hurt in the process!" I went to bed annoyed with Kevin that night.

I got the call about five o'clock that next morning. I fumbled for the phone as my eyes looked over at the clock. "Christine, we have your son here at the department of corrections!" I was trying to focus on what this officer was telling me. "He was brought in a couple of hours ago." He added. I sat up in the bed afraid of what he would say next.

"Marcus was arrested earlier for sexual assault! He will go before the judge later today. At that time they will post his bond." I hung up the phone. Kevin sat there looking at me, "What is wrong Christine?" he said. I started to cry, "Marcus was arrested, and it's my fault Kevin! I should have brought him home last night!" I screamed. "No Christine, whatever he has done, he did it on his own. Don't blame yourself!" he said.

I called Clint later that morning to tell him what had happened. I knew this was going to cost us a fortune. "I'll see if I can find out what his bond is going to be Christine," Clint told me. "I'll call you back as soon as I know." I sat down on the floor in my office, crying for what seemed like hours. I wasn't sure how much more I could handle. Clint called with all the details of the charges against Marc. The bond was more than what I had so he had to sit in jail for a while. It was two weeks before Christmas. Kevin and I decided not to do the holidays that year. Marc called everyday. I tried to comfort him the best that I could. "I want out of here mom," he'd tell me. "I know you do Marc," I'd tell him. "But we are trying to raise your bond money."

Three weeks went by before we got the money to bail Marc out of jail. I was so glad to have him home but at the same time I dreaded it. It was nice not having him around, seeing him drunk all the time. Marcus was verbally abusive to me. For some reason or another I always felt that he didn't know any better. I would make excuses for him and live with the pain.

I kept in touch with Clint from that moment on. "Marcus is going to have to plead guilty Christine," Clint told me on the phone one afternoon. "Marcus admitted everything to the arresting officers, so we will request probation for him."

I told Marc what was going to happen; of course he was back on the drugs and alcohol so he really didn't care. Clint told me I needed to get him into sex offender treatment. I couldn't believe how difficult that was. The months were going by so quickly. Clint kept getting continuances at Marc's court proceedings until we had a few programs in place. Marcus was totally out of control at this time. Kevin and he were fighting more than ever. "Marcus!" I screamed at him. "You are out of jail on a bond that we posted for you! How can you be so disrespectful to us?" All he did was shout profanities at me. "I'm done with him Christine," Kevin told me as he walked out the door, slamming it behind him. I couldn't blame Kevin at all. I would have been gone a long time ago if it had been his son who treated me this way.

I watched Marc stagger up to his room as I sat down on the sofa and cried. "What is my problem?" I thought. "Why do I allow this? Do I feel so guilty about this child's life that I'm giving up my own?" Nothing makes sense anymore. I don't want my son living like this but he won't receive help. I found myself taking him to counselor after counselor. Marc would go into a violent rage; hitting a wall or door causing the counselor to stop seeing him. I was out of options. I would drink so much at night until I would pass out. That was my way of coping!

I was beginning to wonder if Marcus had the problems or if it was me. I had the hardest time letting him be responsible for his own actions. A part of me still wanted to protect him; the other part wanted to beat him. I was now on the emotional roller coaster. Marc had admitted to his wrong doings, but I was blaming his actions on his head injury. Was I right, or did Marc know exactly what he was doing?

One night the phone woke me about 11:30. It was mid November; I could hear sleet hitting the window as I answered the phone. "This is officer," was all I heard. I knew at that moment they had Marc. He went on to say, "We are taking him out to the detention center since he is out on bond." I realized this was the best thing that could have happened to Marc! "What did he do?" I asked afraid of what I'd hear. "We caught him breaking into a vehicle, he had stolen some items." The officer replied. I got off the phone with a feeling of relief. I went back to bed and slept better than I had in months.

The next morning I called Clint to tell him that Marc was taken back to jail the night before for breaking into a car. "You need to leave him there Christine," Clint said. "At least he will be off the streets. He will have time to dry out from the drugs and alcohol." He added. I totally agreed with him. It was just so hard for me knowing he was in jail. I didn't want anyone to hurt him.

HOPE

Marcus spent the next six months in the county detention center. It was a difficult time for all of us. Our visitation with Marc was twice a week for one hour. I dreaded going to the jail. The first night was the hardest for me. The jailers led Kevin and me into a little room that had six stalls with two chairs at each stall. There was a telephone at each stall. They brought Marc into the room. Tears started to burn my eyes as he sat in the stall we were seated in, looking at us through a window. Oh how I wanted to hug him, but I wanted to beat him at the same time. Marcus and I picked up the phones at the same time as I heard his voice, "Hi Mom!" I didn't know what to say. I wanted to yell at him. "Can you get me out of here?" he asked. "No Marcus," I said. "I wouldn't get you out of here even if I could. You're stuck in here until court; that may be a while." I told him. Here comes the lecture, I couldn't help myself! "What were you thinking? You have no reason to steal! It's almost as though you want to be in here!" Marcus wouldn't look at me. "Don't yell at me mom!" he said. I handed the phone to Kevin so I could get a grip. They had some idle chitchat, and then Kevin gave the phone back to me. "Clint will be here to see you in the next couple of days." I told him as we were saying our goodbyes. It was so hard leaving him there.

"He's going to be okay Christine," Kevin told me as we were getting in the car to leave that night. It was a cold, rainy November night. I shivered as I got into the car. "I know, but I'm still worried; I can't help but wonder what is going to become of him." I said. Kevin reassured me, "We need to make sure he knows we are here for him, but he has to learn from his mistakes Christine." I knew deep down Kevin was right! Marcus needed to be in jail! At the same time, my heart ached for him. I wanted to make it all go away. I just didn't know how to do it.

The holidays were slowly approaching. It was December 2003. Kevin and I didn't even talk about the holidays. I was busy working with Clint on Marc's behalf trying to keep him out of prison. I answered the phone one afternoon to hear Clint's voice, "Christine, I want to get a psychological evaluation ordered for Marcus. I'd like to do this as soon as possible!" Where was Clint going with this? "Is this necessary?" I asked him. "We need something to work with Christine, maybe we can find out what is going on with him!" Clint replied. I agreed to let this happen even though I was a bit apprehensive about the outcome.

Clint got the evaluation set up for Marcus. The psychologist went to test Marc at the jail. He divided the testing up into two sessions. When Clint called me with the days and times of the evaluation I informed Marcus right away. I knew how Marc was. A surprise visit from a psychologist would upset him. I wanted him to be fully cooperative! It took a couple of weeks for the test results to come back. I set up a time to meet with Clint. "Christine, you need to read this!" Clint said handing me the evaluation. "It was an excellent evaluation; I think it got to the very core of Marcus. We now have a better idea of what is motivating him." Clint added.

My eyes were glued to the evaluation papers as I read the doctors recommendations. "I feel that with proper counseling and medication Marcus can be rehabilitated. I also recommend that he be place in a highly structured environment such as a residential center for at least ninety days followed by supervised probation." The next statement scared me to death! "Marcus could never survive our prison system!" he added.

The contents of the next page revealed how he came to those conclusions. I could tell Clint was awaiting my response to the information on the next page.

I slowly read the following notes from the doctor. “Marcus has revealed to me that he has been sexually abused by adult men in the past.” I started to get sick! “Did you know about this Christine?” Clint asked me. “No!” I said frantically. “I didn’t know any of this!” I went on reading, “Marcus was molested by a man at gunpoint while living with his father in Georgia. He also felt deserted by his father.” I looked at Clint; my emotions were running wild. I wanted to cry, but at the same time I was so angry! “I’m sure we can get the prosecutor to agree to the terms the doctor has recommended Christine!” Clint told me. I nodded consent but my mind was still on Marc’s father. How could he let these things happen to Marc?

I left Clint’s office that day actually kind of relieved. At least we had some idea of what was going on in Marc’s head. Some of the issues had been identified enabling us to get the right programs in place for his recovery of all this mess. I felt so guilty, sending him to his dad’s. I should have known better! More than ever I was determined to help Marcus get through this. I decided I wasn’t going to say anything to Marc, or his dad, at this time about the information I read in the evaluation.

It was now April 2004. Kevin and I went to visit Marcus a couple of days before our court date. I could tell by the look on his face he was ready to get out of there. “Clint is recommending that you get three years probation on the assault charge. The prosecutor has also agreed to drop all the other theft charges if we pay restitution. You also have to agree to go to a residential center for the first part of your probation.” I told Marc as he glared at me through the glass. “That’s cool,” he said, “I’ve heard about the center Mom, some of the guys in here did time there.” He didn’t sound too excited about it. "We are going to make this work Marc!" I assured him as we were leaving that night.

I was a nervous wreck the morning of court. "Relax Christine; the judge is going to agree with what Clint and the prosecutor have proposed for Marc." Kevin told me. "I know but there is always the chance that the judge won't. He can do whatever he wants." I told Kevin as my hands were shaking. We entered the courtroom. I saw an officer bring Marcus into the courtroom with handcuffs on. This was tearing me up. I sat there looking at him thinking to myself, "Is my baby a criminal? They say he is!" My thoughts were interrupted with the Judge ordering Marcus to be detained at the correctional facility until a bed becomes available at the center. He had granted Marcus his probation.

"Thank You Lord," I said as we were leaving the courtroom. I wasn't sure how God fit into all of this, but I'm almost positive he was right in the middle of it. I wasn't living for him, I had no fellowship with him, but there was a part of me that knew he was there. If not for me, at least he was there for Marc. Kevin and I had hope! We felt as though we had been given another chance to help Marc get his life in order. The judge had spared Marc prison; I would be eternally grateful for that.

About a week later the phone rang. "Hi Mom, I'm here at the center, can you bring me some clothes?" Marc said excitedly. I was so happy to hear his voice. He went on to say, "Visiting here is on the weekends only, but you can come out to bring me the things I need." I felt so relieved. "I'll be there as soon as I can get there," I told him getting off the phone. It didn't take me long to gather up the things that he requested.

The center was about twenty miles outside the city. All I could think about was hugging my baby for the first time in six months. I knew he needed a hug, so did I!

I arrived at the center shortly after lunch that day. I had to show identification at the door. They made me wait in a lobby for Marc. I was so happy to see him. I gave him the biggest hug ever. "This is a copy of the rules and regulations for the center Mom," Marc said handing me a booklet. "I also have a probation officer here, her name is Cindy." He added. A staff member of the center came back out to get Marc so I had to go. "I'll see you Saturday at visitation." I told him as I was leaving. I was anxious to get home to call Marc's probation officer, Cindy. I wanted to tell her about Marc. They also needed to get Marc an appointment at the mental health for his medication. Being in this place with all these rules and regulations, he was going to need them!

The first thing I did when I got home was read the rulebook. I needed to understand what went on there before I called Cindy. I sat down with a cup of coffee that afternoon and began to read. I was worried about Marc making it through the next one hundred twenty days. I knew him! If we were going to make it, I needed to know everything about that place. I started reading about the things that will get a person written up. This wasn't going to be easy. Then I got into the more positive information. "Every person residing at the center will be required to obtain employment," I read. "You are required to also work on your high school diploma or a GED." It said. These were good things. One of Marcus' problems has always been that he has too much time on his hands. I could tell as I familiarized myself with the handbook that they were preparing them for life outside of jail.

I was ready to make the call. "This is Cindy, can I help you?" she said. "Hi Cindy, my name is Christine Huhs, I'm Marcus Bell's mother." I replied. "Yes, Marcus told me you would be calling." She said. I was glad that Marc informed her.

"Marcus battles with depression and anxiety attacks. He really needs to be on medication for this to work." I told her.

She immediately responded, “Yes, I saw that in the probation order, we will get him an appointment at mental health for that.” Cindy and I talked for a little while longer. I felt somewhat better when I got off the phone with her. It was the first of May; Marc had to make it through the end of August.

The next couple of weeks went by rather quickly. Marcus was getting used to his environment. He had a couple of incidences that got him written up. Talking back to the staff members was a big one. I could tell Marc was up and down when he called. It was going on three weeks into the program when I asked, “Have they made the doctors appointment for your medication yet?” I knew he needed it. “No, they haven’t, and they won’t let me go to classes for my GED.” He added. I could hear the frustration in his voice. “I’ll call Cindy tomorrow to see if they have made the appointment.

I did better than that; I scheduled an appointment to meet with her in person. When I arrived at the center I was taken back to Cindy’s office. She was not what I expected at all. She was a petite woman about Marcus’ age. “I came to talk about Marc getting his medication,” I said looking her over. “Marcus has an appointment in two weeks at mental health. Sometimes it takes a while to get in there.” She said. I was the one frustrated at this time, “Five weeks to get him on medication that was court ordered, amazing!” I thought. “Marcus also informed me that he was not allowed to attend any GED classes, is there a reason for that?” I asked her. “We feel that with Marc’s behavioral issues; being disrespectful to staff members etc.; that this would not be a good time.” She answered. I knew at that moment we were not going to make it through this program.

The second week of June finally arrived. Marc got to his doctors’ appointment so they could get him on the medication he needed. We had ten weeks to go before Marc could come home. I got a call from Marc one night, "I got wrote up today for making a racial remark outside." He chuckled. "What? What did you say Marc?" I asked him. "I said the "N" word; we were all standing around rapping. One of the staff members walked by and heard me." I yelled, "Dang it Marcus! Are you ever going to learn?" He got quiet for a moment then said, "Cindy made me sign a behavioral form, that if I get anymore write ups I will go back to jail." I could see it coming. We were down to eight weeks left.

The following Tuesday night I got a call from Marcus. A collect call, so I knew what that meant. "Cindy filed a motion to revoke my probation Mom; I'm back at the county jail." I was disgusted but at the same time I knew it was coming. Marc was upset so I didn't stay on the phone very long with him. I would get so depressed talking to him that it took all that I had within me to hold a conversation with him.

The next morning I was back in Clint's office. "If Cindy filed a motion to revoke his probation Christine, then they will be recommending that he finish out his three year sentence." I couldn't believe what I was hearing. "The staff at the center is not trained to deal with someone like Marc," I told Clint. "What am I going to do with this kid?" Clint adjusted his reading glasses to give me a sympathetic glare. I knew he didn't know what to say. I didn't know what else to do. Court was schedule for November 2004; Marcus would have to sit in the county jail for another four months so we could work this issue out. I left Clint's office crying. I knew I had to try to make sense of all of this.

"The last five years of my life have been ridiculous," I thought as I was driving home from Clint's office. "But then again, my whole life up to this point makes no sense." I just kept driving and thinking! "Marcus isn't a criminal!" I reassured myself. "Oh God, where are you?" I had horrible thoughts of Marcus committing suicide. I don't know how he made it from day to day! I arrived home a couple hours later.

I felt like I needed to get on my knees. But I couldn't! I didn't know how to pray anymore. Marcus' life was totally in God's hands now; I knew this. I wanted to live for the Lord but everything was against me! I was living in sin and I knew that sin separated me from God. I was clueless on how to find my way back to the Lord.

As time went by I kept trying to maintain a positive attitude hoping that the judge would give us another chance. I wanted to bring him home badly! One afternoon Kevin came home from work a little early. I fixed us a cocktail as we headed out the back door for our deck. I loved sitting out there; it was so peaceful. Kevin and I would just talk while we were sipping our drinks. "I would really like to start going to church!" I heard Kevin say. I couldn't believe it; I was astonished! Excitement rose up in me just hearing those words. I felt Kevin could see it in my face. "Sure, let's go," I told him, "I know of one not too far from here that Lee and I had visited a few years ago. It's a good church; I'd like to go Kevin." It had been almost six years since I had been inside a church! What would it be like? Will we be welcomed? What will I wear? What was God thinking about me at that moment? I felt embarrassed to say the least but I wanted to go more than anything in the world. Isn't it funny how these little things seemed so important? We decided to go that Sunday morning.

Sunday morning came so quickly. The anticipation was killing me. I sat on our sofa waiting for the time to leave. I was scared. All of a sudden I didn't want to go. "We're going Christine," as Kevin took my hand leading me towards the door. "We need this!" he said as I got into the car. I knew he was right. Kevin and I walked in the door being greeted by a nice lady. She handed us both a church bulletin as we headed for the main sanctuary. "Wow, this is nice," I thought as Kevin found us a seat. I felt peace, once again, that old familiar peace that I felt back in 1986. I felt like I had stepped into a comfort zone.

The praise and worship time was very nice. I didn't really participate. I wanted to cry but fought back my tears. I looked over at Kevin. He was clapping his hands, singing with a big smile on his face. He seemed to fit right in with all of these people. Kevin had never been in a church like this. It was new to him. We both listened to the pastor as he welcomed sinners to receive Jesus. It sure brought back memories watching people go forward to receive their salvation. Then came "If you've been apart from the Lord and you want to come back, he is waiting with open arms to receive you!" I could hardly stand still! My spirit came alive!

Before we knew it the service was over. Kevin could hardly contain himself on the ride home. "That was awesome Christine," he said. "I want to go back on Wednesday." I smiled. I couldn't wait to get home!

WHO DO WE TRUST?

Kevin pulled the car into the garage and I jumped out hardly waiting for him to park. I ran into the house and downstairs to the basement where I knew I had boxes of old church teaching tapes and videos packed away. I couldn't wait to get my hands on them! I anxiously pulled them out, box after box, going through them like a child with a new box of toys! Kevin glared at me like I had lost my mind. "These teaching tapes are very old Kevin, I sure hope they play." I told him, as I looked them over. "Where did you get these? He asked looking at some that were at least twenty years old. "I had acquired them from people over the years. A lot of these are from Pastor Varney's services back in Topeka. Every one of the tapes played. Kevin and I were excited about the month's worth of teaching we were about to receive.

Marcus called that Sunday night. "Kevin and I went to church this morning." I told him. "That's cool Mom, I'd like to go with you guys when I get home. I'm really done with all the drugs Mom, I'm not going back to that stuff when I get home." He said. I really believed him. I got off the phone with Marc feeling more depressed than usual. I needed a drink! But I just couldn't get myself to fix one. I worried about Marc behind bars; that someone might hurt him. I always wanted to take his pain but I didn't know how. I'd cry myself to sleep and part of me would hope that I wouldn't wake up the next morning. The other part of me knew I had to for Marcus' sake. I lay in bed that night hoping that when I woke in the morning this nightmare would be over. Little did I know the battle had just begun!

The next morning was a dreadful one. It was a rainy, dreary, cold Monday morning in October. We had about six weeks before Marc's court hearing. I felt awful that morning. I can't describe the sick feeling in the pit of my stomach. I knew I needed to talk to someone, I felt as though I were losing my mind! I was losing control! I was standing in my bedroom, looking out the window when all of a sudden I fell to my knees! "Oh God, what have I done? Please help me!" I cried. "I can't do this; I can't do this any more!" I put my face down in my hands as I sobbed. I felt totally helpless! The next thing I knew, I was having a heart to heart talk with Jesus. I laid every thing on the table. I told him all that I had done, that I could remember anyway. I realized that he already knew but I felt that he wanted to hear it from me.

I asked Jesus to forgive me. I needed his love and support like never before. I gave my life to him that day. Our talk changed my life forever! I asked Jesus to come into my heart back in 1986, but I never surrendered my life to him. I was reminded of a passage of scripture that day. "For we have not a high priest which cannot be touched with the feeling of our infirmities; but was in all points tempted like as we are, yet without sin. Let us therefore come boldly to the throne of grace, that we may obtain mercy, and find grace to help in time of need." (Heb. 4:15, 16)

I had a fabulous time with Jesus that day. I laughed and cried at the same time. I praised him with all that I had within me. I felt burdens lifting off my shoulders. I gave the Lord my pain, my family, my worries, my doubts, my insecurities, but most of all, my heart! In return he gave me hope, love, peace, joy, security and a confidence that made me know that every thing was going to be all right! I once heard a preacher say, "The Lord is married to the backslider." How true that statement is!

I was amazed at how quickly Kevin was learning about the Lord. We spent most of our evenings with our bibles listening to the teaching tapes. My prayer life was changing. The scriptures that I had learned many years ago would start flowing out of my mouth. It was so exciting! I felt a strength and boldness come over me like I had never experienced. I found myself praying the Word of God! I would speak the scriptures that pertained to my life and my circumstances.

I craved the Word of God! The scriptures had come alive to me! I was receiving revelation of his word like I had never experienced. I saw it literally changing our lives. Kevin and I had been through hell; we had nearly lost everything! It was time for restoration in our families and in our finances. I really believed God and held him at his word!

It was a couple of weeks before Marcus' court appearance. I had peace in my heart but I still had to meet with Clint. I was going to fight every inch of the way to keep Marc out of prison. "The Judge will do what he wants to do Christine. I can propose to the district attorney that Marc be hospitalized but I don't think you want that." He said. "If he goes to prison he will get credit for the time he has already served." Clint had placed our options on the table. I left his office that afternoon wondering what the Lord was doing here. Clint made it seem like taking Marcus home was out of the question.

I prayed and still didn't know what to do. "Tell Clint you want to talk to the Judge Christine!" Kevin told me a few days before court. "Tell the Judge you want to bring Marc home!" he added. Why didn't I think of that? I immediately went back to see Clint. Court was on Friday morning that week so I only had a couple of days to convince Clint to get the Judge to hear me. "What do you want to happen here Christine?" Clint asked me.

I want to talk to the Judge to reassure him that I will take care of Marcus at home! That's what I want to happen!"

Clint sighed, slightly shaking his head in doubt, "Okay, we'll give it a try!" I left Clint's office feeling very confident.

Friday morning, November 12, 2004 had finally arrived. I was dreading it. At the same time I wanted it to be over. This was Marc's last chance. If the Judge didn't let me take him home, he was going to prison. My hands were trembling as Kevin and I walked into the courtroom with Clint. The staff from the residential center was there. "They will get to talk to the Judge first Christine; they are going to recommend that he go to prison and serve his sentence." Clint said hesitantly, knowing how I felt about this prison thing. I didn't have bad feelings for anyone at the center; I just knew they couldn't handle Marcus. The Judge finally entered the room. I was scared to death, I felt as though I were the one being sentenced. When the prosecutor finished his remarks to the Judge, Clint finally spoke up. "Your honor, Marcus' mother, Christine Huhs would like to address the court." I stood to my feet, pulling every ounce of strength I could from the Lord, "Help me Jesus!" I whispered. "Help me to convince this Judge that we can do this." I looked at the Judge sitting there with a solemn look on his face as he waited patiently for me to speak.

My voice trembled "Your honor, my husband and I feel that we can help Marc complete his probation successfully at home with us. We will be his supervisors, making sure he keeps all appointments and we will monitor his medications as well." The Judge sat there in silence for a few seconds then said, "I need the weekend to think this over." My heart sank. "God, what are you doing here, why do we have to wait over the weekend?" I asked. I was a little confused but I knew I had to trust in the Lord. "We will resume at two o'clock Monday afternoon." The Judge added.

I knew in my heart now was no time to be questioning God. I stood firm all weekend knowing that it was God's will that Marc be home with us. Kevin and I didn't discuss court at all the entire weekend. We didn't want to confess anything negative about Marc's situation.

Monday afternoon finally arrived. "I'm going to release Mr. Bell to his parents." I heard the Judge say. That was all I heard. It was so awesome, "Thank you Jesus, so much!" What a victory! Later that afternoon I drove out to the correctional facility where they had Marc. They were releasing him. It normally took a couple of hours before Marc came out to the waiting area. I couldn't wait to see him. Finally he was released. He gave me a big hug, "Thanks Mom," he said as we headed to the car. On our ride home the reality of this probation set in. Marc was on supervised probation, which literally meant that he couldn't be out of our sight. This was going to be interesting!

It was great having Marcus home! The next morning we had to meet with his new probation officer for the first time. Her name was Sara. Marc wasn't crazy about her but I liked her. "I'll need to see you six times a month." She said as she handed Marc and I a copy of his probation orders. We had about eight months of his probation behind us with another two years and four months to go. "Hope I can do this Marcus!" I told him as we got in the car. "We can do this Mom, it will be easy." He assured me. I knew I would have no life for the next two years, but I made an agreement with the Judge and I was determined to keep my end of the deal. God knew that I could do this. I thank him for being in that courtroom with me, and by his grace we will succeed.

Christmas of 2004 was the best we ever had. Kevin and I were so broke but it didn't matter. I could sleep at night knowing Marc was in the room across the hall from us.

Alysan and Conner just had a birthday. Aly turned eight years old and Conner turned six. Conner loved his uncle Marcus. They would entertain one another. Joni brought the kids to see us on Christmas Day. Daniel was seeing another girl by this time, but he did manage to stop by. I loved my children so much and having them home was a real blessing.

I got very bored at times. Marc always wanted to go somewhere. One Saturday afternoon he talked me in to going to the movies. "Come on Mom, let's go, it will get us out of the house for a while." He said. Kevin was working that Saturday so I agreed. When the movie let out Marc made a dash to the snack bar. I stood by the door waiting while he got his drink. I saw him talking to a female cashier. After a few minutes I saw them exchange phone numbers. I decided not to lecture him. He needed some companionship, besides his mother! "Her name is Mindy, I got her phone number!" he said excitedly. "I'm going to call her tonight!" I just looked at him, "Just be careful Marc, you know how these females are!" I told him. I couldn't believe what I was saying; I was being so judgmental.

During the next couple of weeks Marc was on the phone constantly with Mindy. She was calling him as much as he was calling her. I was glad for him because he had someone to talk to. "She's so nice Mom, not like most of the girls out there." He told me. "Can we go to the theater this Saturday?" he asked. "She doesn't have to work so we can spend some time together." I didn't feel real good about this. "I'll talk to Kevin about it and let you know." I answered. "It will be okay. Mindy even wants to meet Sara so that she can be a supervisor for me." Marc added. I had this fear of Marc around females and I knew I had to get over it. "I think it's a great idea Christine, lets take him to the movies and meet her. If she likes Marc, that's a positive thing for him." Kevin said trying to convince me. "We have to let him be a man," he added. I had to admit, I wanted a close up of this girl so we decided to take him.

Saturday afternoon when we arrived at the theater Mindy was waiting at the door for Marc. "This is Mindy!" Marc said proudly as he introduced us. I had to admit she wasn't what I had hoped for Marcus but I decided to give her the benefit of the doubt. “Mindy wants to see this movie mom; we don’t want to see the one you and Kevin are going to see.” Marc said as we were standing in line for popcorn. Oh no, here it comes. Do we say no, and risk a scene right there in the lobby of the theater? Or do we allow him to violate his probation? “Kevin, I think Marc needs to come with us.” I said quickly and quietly. “Mom, nothing is going to happen,” Marc said. “I think it will be okay Christine, we can go in and check on them from time to time.” Kevin said interrupting Marc and me.

Kevin and I went in to the theater across the hall from Marc and Mindy. I felt sick to my stomach. I knew Kevin and I were the violators here. We were just as much to blame as Marc. The movie finally let out. It couldn’t have ended soon enough for me. Marc and Mindy were already out in the snack bar area sitting at a table talking. “Marc, it’s time to go.” Kevin said as we approached their table. Marc gave her a hug and we headed for the door. She was smiling and waving at him so I guess every thing went okay. The next day Marc asked me for Sara’s phone number. “Mindy is going to call her for an appointment to meet her so she can supervise me. Then I can go places with Mindy.” Marc said. I agreed and gave him the number. We had an appointment with Sara on Tuesday and Marc told her about Mindy. Sara thought it was great that Marc had a girlfriend. “Mindy is going to call you for an appointment soon.” Marc told Sara as we were leaving. I don’t think I ever saw Marcus so happy! Even though he didn’t get to see her, he was crazy about her. They still spent hours on the phone.

The next Tuesday Marc had his appointment with Sara. As we were getting up to leave Sara said, “I still haven’t heard from Mindy.” Marc turned around and told her, “She doesn’t have transportation right now; she is getting ready to buy a new car. She said she would make the appointment as soon as she could get here.” I didn’t think much of it at that moment; all I knew was that I wasn't volunteering anything. If she wanted to meet Sara, she would have to get there on her own.

Another week went by with Marc on cloud nine. It was Valentines Day! "Mom, can you take me to get a card for Mindy? I'd like to take it to her at the theater, she is working today." Marc said. I took Marc to the store where we picked her out a lovely card. Then we went to the theater. I let Marc go inside; I stood by the window where I could see them. They sat down at a table as she opened the card. I could see the smile on her face as she hugged him. I opened the door and told Marc, "It's time to go." I really was happy for him.

One night later that week, I was in my office when Marc came in and sat down. I knew something was horribly wrong. "What's the matter?" I asked, afraid of his response. "I just called Mindy. Her room mate said that she moved out!" he exclaimed. "Moved out? Where did she go?" I asked. "She moved in with her boyfriend!" he yelled. "I thought I was her boyfriend Mom!" My heart sank. I felt so bad for him. I could see the pain on his face. He was so hurt! Marc stormed out of my office and I heard his bedroom door shut. I didn't know what to say to him. I went downstairs and told Kevin what happened. "Leave him alone Christine, this is part of life, he has to learn to deal with these things. He will be okay." Kevin told me.

The next few days were rather quiet around the house. It came time for our appointment with Sara. When it came time for us to leave Sara inquired about Mindy again. Marc said, "She won't be calling you after all." I just shook my head at Sara and she dropped it. I was glad she didn't keep asking Marc about it. He was still upset.

I got a call from my niece Sharon, who lives in Pennsylvania. She wanted to bring her family to Kansas City for a visit. I was so excited to have them come. They were coming the second week in March. I told her it would probably still be cold and rainy but they wanted to come anyway. Marcus and I got the guest room ready for Sharon's visit. Marc was excited because he had never met her. We had another appointment with Sara the day before Sharon was due to arrive. Sara took us back to the room we always met in. As we were all sitting down she said, "I talked to Mindy." Marc and I both looked at her surprised because Marc had not talked to her in about 3 weeks. "She said that she didn't want to see you again because she was afraid of you Marcus." She added. Marcus immediately became defensive. He stood up yelling at Sara. I told him to be quiet and sit down. Then Sara looked at me, "Mindy also said that Marc was at the theater unsupervised. There was another witness there that saw Marc get dropped off, walking through the parking lot alone." I was shocked at these allegations. I knew that Marc had done nothing to this girl. I saw them together the last time he was with her. She did not look like a girl afraid of him. It was Valentine's Day.

Then Sara hit us with the news. "I talked to Judge this morning and we have agreed it would be best for Marc to be placed on house arrest." Marcus was fighting mad! He stormed out of her office. "I'm sorry Christine, but I had to tell the Judge. This is for his protection as well as anyone else." I sat there in shock. "I understand Sara, you have to do your job, but this girl is lying about all of this." Marc went back out to the waiting room while I finished the conversation with Sara. I couldn't believe this was happening. Kevin and I had sacrificed everything to ensure that Marcus made it through this probation. I was so hurt. "I had to file a motion to revoke his probation Christine. We will get a court date and go before the Judge to prove our innocence." I couldn't understand any of this. I left Sara's office with instructions on how to get the house arrest equipment. I had to take Marc back out to the residential center where he had spent two months last summer. He dreaded going in there. I felt so bad for him. Marc spent nearly three hours in there while I sat out in the car waiting for him. They wouldn't allow me to accompany him. "This is stupid Mom!" Marc said as he open the car door. I had never seen an ankle bracelet before. "What a gadget," I thought as he was getting in the car. He had a bag of equipment with directions on how to hook it all up to your phone line with it. I was sick, so was Marcus!

Thirty minutes later we arrived home. Marcus took the equipment upstairs to his bedroom and I followed. Marc proceeded to get the equipment set up as I read the installation instructions. After a few minutes it was ready to go. There was a monitor with a button on the right side of it. When the phone rang he only had three to four rings to answer. Once he answered the phone, a recorded voice told him to hold up a certain amount of fingers, or to put his finger on his nose, etc. Then he pushed a button that took his picture. This was devastating to me. Not only was Marcus on house arrest, so were we! I was so angry with this girl for what she had done. I had to be very careful for the way I felt about Mindy because I knew the consequences for unforgiveness. So I decided to roll this burden over on to the Lord. It was too much for me to handle! Marc had to be at the center once a week to meet with the house arrest officer and still keep his appointments with Sara.

The first night with this phone monitor was a disaster. Kevin and I knew the phone had to be answered every time it rang or police officers would be knocking at our door. House arrest called every two hours all through the night. Marcus was on medication that would make him sleepy so he wouldn't even hear the phone. Kevin and I would go into Marc's room and I would answer the phone while Kevin would stand Marc up in front of the monitor to take his picture. This went on for several nights. Kevin and I couldn't take any more. I finally got to get out of the house. We had an appointment with Sara. "Kevin and I can't take these calls all night long!" I told her. "Either we are going to have to change Marc's medications or they are going to have to stop all of these calls." I don't know what she did but the nighttime calls got less and less.

I'm not sure why all of this happened to us, I may never know. I did know that God would turn all of this around. Sitting at home on house arrest with Marc I decided it was time for me to get some help. I loved Marcus dearly but it was time for me to find resources that could help Marc. I wasn't worried about the court over this incident; I truly felt we had done nothing wrong. It was the next two years I was worried about. "How am I ever going to make it through the next two years Lord?" I thought. I had a peace within myself that every thing was going to be okay.

Our next visit with Sara was very nice. "We need to get Marc some counseling Christine," she told me. "One of the other officers here has a client that goes to the Rehabilitation Institute. Here is the phone number if you'd like to call them to see what they offer." I smiled as we got up to leave, "Thank You Sara," I said taking the number from her. "I'll call them today."

Marc still had a real bad attitude about this house arrest thing. I tried to get him to be quiet when we were in Sara's office. One thing about Marc, he loves to voice his opinion!

I couldn't wait to get home and call the Rehabilitation Institute. I had a list of names so I just picked one out. "Could I speak to Dr. Marshall please?" I asked the receptionist. I was on hold for a quite a while as I thought about what I would say. "This is Dr. Marshall," I heard interrupting my thoughts, "how may I help you?" I decided the best thing to do was to start from the beginning. I knew the root of our problems were Marc's head injury and tracheotomy. Finishing my story I heard her say, "I'd love to work with Marcus! Since he is on Medicaid it will probably be about six months before we can see him." That was disappointing but I made the appointment with her anyway. It gave us something to look forward to. "Christine, I think it would benefit Marcus and your family for you to contact a community service. They provide services to head injury patients. From what you've told me Marcus would probably qualify for a head injury waiver." She told me. "I've used a community service before Dr. Marshall, it ended in disaster." I said. She hesitated for a moment then said, "You think about it and if you decide to give them another try call Sheryl Brown. She's a great lady; I think they can help." Okay, I'll think about it." I told her as we hung up the phone.

My niece Sharon and her family arrived at our house on a Thursday. We couldn't really do anything but it sure was nice to have someone to talk to besides Marcus. I was so tired of looking at him! On Friday morning Marcus had a doctor's appointment for his medications. We also had to stop by the pharmacy to fill his prescriptions. I was so tired that day, not feeling real good. I wanted to go outside to enjoy Sharon and Archie's' company while they were sitting on the deck watching their children playing in the back yard.

It was a beautiful day, sunny and warm. I decided to go upstairs and try to take a nap before dinner. I walked in to the kitchen, dropped Marc's prescription bags on the kitchen counter and went upstairs. About an hour went by. I was just resting, when Sharon was knocking on my door. "Aunt Christine, Marcus is acting really strange downstairs; you might want to check on him. He was outside with us and fell off the deck steps." I jumped up and got to my feet, trying to get my balance, "Oh Lord, what has he done?" I remember going over in my mind, "We have no liquor in the house; he hasn't been out where he could have gotten a hold of any drugs." I came around the corner seeing Marc standing at the refrigerator, wobbling back and forth. My eyes scanned the kitchen, oh no, his medicine bag was open. "Marcus!" I screamed, "What have you done?" I grabbed the bag, opened a bottle and started counting. "There are ten missing

Marcus!" Still screaming at him I opened the second of three bottles. "Sharon, would you please help Marc upstairs to his room?" I asked as I counted seven more missing pills. I threw the bottles down on the counter so that I could assist Sharon. Marc was becoming delirious. It was hard to hold him up but we finally got him to his room. I made him sit down on the edge of his bed. I just looked at him in disgust as he sat there with a big grin on his face. All of a sudden he fell back, passed out.

Hysterically I started rambling, "What do I do? Who do I call? Surely this is a probation violation!" Sharon glared at me, "Aunt Christine, maybe you should call the poison control center, they can tell you what to do." She was right, "Okay, then I'm going to have to call Sara and the house arrest officer." Sharon ran downstairs to get the other bottle of pills so that I would have an accurate count of what he took. I called the poison control center. "You need to call him an ambulance; sometimes they fall into a deep sleep and forget to breathe." The lady on the phone told me.

"Oh God help me, Lord keep Marc breathing!" I prayed as I called Kevin at work. "I need you to come home quickly," I told him, "Marcus got into his medicine and has passed out. I'm calling an ambulance honey, please hurry!" I got off the phone and sat down on the bed beside Marcus. Kevin pulled up about the same time the ambulance did. There were two police officers with the medics. The medics were taking Marc out the front door on a stretcher. I couldn't help but cry. "Is he on house arrest?" one of the officers asked looking right at Marc's ankle bracelet. "Yes, he is," I stated. "I need to call them." I glanced over at Kevin talking to a medic as they put Marc in to the ambulance. Kevin walked towards me, "We are going to meet them at the hospital Christine, let's go." I was frightened, "What if Marc really hurt himself this time?" I thought to myself getting in the car. On the way to the hospital I called house arrest and Sara.

I had to leave Sara a message since it was a Friday evening. I knew she wouldn't be in her office.

Once Kevin and I got to the hospital we found Marc in the intensive care unit. The nurses had all kinds of questions. I knew the routine so well. I hated it there. I hated hospitals with a passion. "I think he is going to be okay, we will keep him for a few days to monitor him." A nurse told me. "You might as well go home," I told Kevin, "I'll stay here and see you in the morning." He agreed. It was a long night! I kept talking to Marc hoping he would wake up. The next morning a hospital psychiatrist came by to see me. "Do you think Marc was trying to commit suicide?" she asked. I looked up at her and started laughing. "Is that what you guys think? No way! Marc was trying to get a buzz! He just over did it." I told her. She started to walk away, "I'll be back to talk to him when he wakes up."

I was so glad to see Kevin walking in the room. "How is he?" he asked. "He's still sleeping; I need to get a cup of coffee and get out of this room." I told him.

As Kevin and I headed for the elevator I told him of my conversation with the psychiatrist. He laughed! Kevin and I knew Marcus very well. He had a life! Not much of one at the moment but he was always very positive about where he was going. Deep down inside I knew Marc was going to be okay. God has had his hand on Marcus since the day he was born. He had work for Marc to do. My heart told me that God would finish the work he started in him. I really wasn't sure what the work was but Marc was sure it was music. He wrote his lyrics all the time then walked around the house rapping them. I can still hear him saying, "I'm going to be a rapper mom, and I'm going to be famous!"

Later that afternoon I was standing at the foot of Marc's bed when he woke up. "What am I doing here?" he asked with a smile on his face. I couldn't help but laugh. "Thank You

Jesus," I said walking around to the side of the bed. "Marcus, what were you thinking taking all of those pills? You could have seriously hurt yourself!" I said. "I just wanted to get some sleep without hearing the phone ring." He told me. I knew how he felt, I had thought of taking a few of them myself. We couldn't get any sleep at our house while Marc was on house arrest. Court wasn't for another six weeks so we had to get used to this thing.

COURT AGAIN

Kevin and I took Marc home from the hospital late Sunday afternoon. "I'm sure you are going to receive a probation violation for this stunt Marc." I told him as we were getting in the car. Marc's attitude at this time was bad. "I might as well be in prison Mom!" he shouted at me. "Stop it Marc, we've come too far to give up now." I told him getting very angry at his attitude. "House arrest is worse than prison!" he yelled. It was a nightmare but I knew we would get through it. At least we were all home.

On Tuesday we went to see Sara. I was afraid of what was going to happen to Marc but she never said anything. I was shocked! When we arrived at home later I decided it was time for me to get some real help. I called Sheryl Brown at the community service that Dr. Marshall requested. She came over the next day to meet us. We discovered that they no longer employed most of the people with the service. I liked her. I gave Sheryl all of the information she requested. "I'll submit this information to see if Marc still qualifies for the head injury waiver. I'll get back to you as soon as I hear anything." She said as she was going out the door. Marc headed for the stairs; I could tell he wasn't real excited about this. I was determined to get some help. I wanted to give them a try.

It was time for Sharon and Archie to leave. I felt so bad about this being their family vacation, being stuck in the house with Marc and me. She understood our situation with Marc. I was so glad she came to visit; she entertained Marcus a lot. Marcus would entertain them with his rapping, which drove me crazy! "I hate to see you go Sharon, I'm sorry we didn't get to do anything," I told her as they were leaving. "Don't worry about it Aunt Christine, we got to get out of Pennsylvania for a while and it was good to see you, Marc, and Kevin." She said.

I stood at the door, waving goodbye as they drove off. Sharon made me homesick. I wanted to go home. As weird as it may seem, as much as I hated it there, I think a part of me needed to go there once in a while. I'd like driving down the main street of my hometown and imagine my dad walking down the street. It would make me smile. As I said before, some of the memories were good.

The phone ringing as I watch Sharon and Archie drive off startled me. I closed the door and went to answer it. "Christine, this is Sheryl Brown calling." She said. "Wow that was fast." I thought. "I heard back concerning the head injury waiver and Marc was approved for services." She added. I wanted to jump for joy! "I'm going to assign Marcus a case manager who will be getting in touch with you in the next few days. Her name is Karen Dalton." She said as my mind was trying to keep up with her words. All I could see at that moment was light at the end of this dark tunnel we were in. "Thank you Sheryl, I really appreciate you doing this for us!" I told her. I called Marc and Kevin in to the kitchen and told them the news. Kevin was okay with the idea but Marc was apprehensive. I couldn't blame him though, I was a little nervous about the entire thing. I knew we needed help and I was grabbing a hold of anything I could get my hands on. Two years had gone by since we used the community service; I kept convincing myself they had improved.

I despised being on house arrest. Everyday was a challenge. Marc was hard to live with let alone being locked up with him twenty-four hours a day. I spent a lot of time in my room. I prayed that God was going to turn this around also. It often amazed me at the inner peace that I had. I knew it was coming from him. I was learning more about the Lord. I read the bible all the time and started to learn some of God's ways. How awesome he is!

Karen Dalton from the community service called and scheduled a meeting with Marc and me. We only had about three weeks before court. I knew we had to get some programs in place for Marc before we went before the judge, again! I was really tired of going to court.

Karen was terrific! She was very straightforward with Marc and me. "The past is the past," she said, "Our job is to help Marc with his future!" I loved this lady, she thought like I did. Karen assigned Marcus a TLS (transitional living specialist), who would work with Marcus a few hours a week. They would work on things such as simple living skills, behaviors, etc. Of course we all had to meet with Sara. Since the TLS would be spending time alone with Marc and taking him out in to the community, it required Sara's approval. I was in heaven. I would get a few hours a week of free time.

Sara was very optimistic about the plans we wanted to put in to action for Marc. "I will write up the plan and submit it to the prosecutor and the judge before our court date." She told us. Kevin and I were so happy; God was truly working on our behalf. It was time once again for court. The judge agreed with everything Sara proposed. It was May 30, 2005 and we were getting off house arrest. I drove Marc out to the center to return his equipment. We were so happy to see that stuff go!

A couple of days went by before Karen introduced us to Melvin, the TLS they assigned to Marc. "Christine," Karen said, "Its time for you to get back to the role of Mom instead of caregiver." I knew deep down she was right. That afternoon was wonderful. Melvin and Marcus worked on a goal sheet. "What are your goals Marcus? What would you like to see happen in your life in the future?" Melvin asked Marc. I looked over at Marc and could see a glimpse of hope on his face for the first time.

"I want to get my GED." Marc said. "That's most important if I am going to get a good job." I was so proud of him at that moment. "I want to finish my album, I want to spend more time at the studio." He continued. I knew that was coming! That's all Marc talked about, the studio and his music. I couldn't blame him; he put all he had in to the album that he started four years earlier.

Marc was with Melvin three days a week for a couple of hours each day. It was wonderful for me. I had some free time to think about Kevin and me. Marc was a full time job. I know I have neglected my husband, and myself for that matter. It was time for me to seek out a part time job. "I think I can find a job at a salon." I told Kevin one night over dinner. "I need one that will let me work a few hours in the evenings." Kevin looked relieved, "That would get you some badly needed time away from the house," he said, "And we sure could use some extra money coming in." I couldn't agree more.

This was something I knew the Lord would take care of. I took it to him in prayer that he would lead me to the right place. I called a salon that was close to home to see if they were hiring. "You can come in and fill out an application." The lady told me over the phone. I decided this one afternoon while Marc was gone with Melvin that I would go. I walked in and there was a lady that took me back to a break room. "Fill this out and then we can talk." She said. I filled out the application and went over in my mind about what I would tell her about my situation. I knew at that moment the Lord was putting it on my heart, "Tell the truth!"

I finished filling out the application and she sat down across the table from me as she introduced herself. "I'm Julie, one of the owners of the salon." She said taking my application.

I went over everything with her. Julie was awesome! "The manager is on vacation this week but I will tell her to put you on the next schedule." She told me as she wrote down my availability. "You'll like the manager here, she is a great lady to work for." She told me as I got up to leave. "Call her on Friday for your schedule, you can start next week." She added. I was so excited I could hardly wait to call Kevin with the news of my new job.

I had so much to be grateful for! Marc was doing much better; his attitude towards life was more positive than it had ever been. I had a new job! God was bringing us out of the hole we had been trapped in for so long. I knew God had a plan and purpose for our lives; I was still clueless of what that purpose was.

Marcus walked in the door one afternoon with Melvin behind him. "Mom, check this out." He said with excitement in his voice. "Melvin found me an agent that I can send my album to for them to find me a record label." He was talking so fast I could hardly understand what he was saying. "I have to mail them a check for four hundred dollars along with a copy of my music." He added handing me an envelope. "Can you mail this for me?" he asked. I had a lot of questions before I let Marc mail four hundred dollars off to a strange company. "I will mail it for you but before we do this I think we should check this company out." I told him. "They have a website Christine, here is the address!" Melvin interceded. "Okay, we will look this over Marc, then we will mail it. I think we should check the better business bureau also to find out more about their business practices, okay?" I asked, directing my question to Marcus. He agreed.

Later that day Marcus and I got on the computer and found this companies' website. It looked legitimate so we then checked them out with the better business bureau.

We were satisfied with our findings so we mailed the envelope. "I'm really excited for you Marcus!" I told him. He smiled, "I know this is what I'm going to do with my life Mom, God brought me this far, we are going all the way!" he told me, so confident in his words. I couldn't help but think about all that we had been through his entire life. "Is this it Lord?" I thought. "Please don't let him down, I don't think any of us could handle another major disappointment in our lives." I began to pray everyday for Marc to get a record label. I believed he would be offered one but my lack of knowledge in the music business made me wonder if it was going to be worth it!

I was working at the salon a couple of evenings a week and on the weekends. I loved my job and the people I worked with. What a blessing! One Saturday afternoon in the fall of 2005 I was at work when Kevin and Marc stopped by the salon to see me. "Your not going to believe what just happened Christine," Kevin said hardly catching his breath. "There is a huge garage sale at the church down the street so Marc and I decided to stop." He added. "Marc was talking to the youth pastor and he was intrigued with him having a tracheotomy! Then Marc showed him his album." I stood there looking at the both of them wondering where they were going with this. "Mom," Marc said, "They asked me to come and perform at their church!" I could hardly believe what I was hearing. Marcus and Kevin were so excited. "When is this going to happen?" I asked. "Tomorrow night!" Kevin stated as they were leaving because I had to get back to work.

I went back inside the salon amazed. I told everyone I came in contact with about my son performing at the church. I could hardly wait for Sunday night to get here. I wanted to see this more than anyone. "Was he going to be able to perform?" I thought. "Was his trach going to hinder him in any way?"

THE LABEL

With Marc pursuing a record label, we definitely needed to see if he could hold up. Marc had to put his finger over his trach when he talked to push the air out of his mouth to make a sound. How would he do this while on stage in front of a lot of people? We were finally about to find out.

Sunday night finally arrived and we anxiously drove to the church. I was impressed with the amount of people who showed up to hear Marc rap. I don't particularly like rap music but this was different.

I watched Marcus strut up to the platform when they introduced him. I was so proud; this was my baby. I reflected back on our lives. I could see him lying in that hospital bed nearly twenty years ago, without a trace of hope, till David walked in to our lives and introduced us to Jesus, the healer. I remembered the doctor's words, "He has a twisted brain stem, and it almost always takes their life!" Little did we know, God had a plan and purpose for Marc and I was about to see it all unravel.

I was so proud as I listened to him performing "Thuggin for Christ"! It's a great song and he did it so well. "He has so much talent!" Kevin told me as he sat in amazement watching Marcus in front of all those people. It was like he was in a world all his own. I had another confirmation that God wasn't finished with the work he started in my son. Marc was going down the road God had chosen for him. I will never carry another burden for Marc. I've rolled him over to the Lord. I have no worries or anxieties. I have total peace because I do know we are in the Lords hands.

Christmas was approaching and I was happy that Daniel was bringing Aly and Conner to spend a few days over the holiday with us. Dan worked a lot and with our schedules we didn't get to see much of our grandchildren. They were growing up so fast. Marc was doing well with the community service and enjoyed his time with Melvin. I was enjoying my free time at work.

The months started going by since Marc mailed a copy of his music to the agent. "These people are not going to find me a label Mom," Marc told me one night. The contract says they have six months to get me a label or they have to pay me back my four hundred dollars." I could tell he was getting impatient but I tried to convince him this sort of thing takes time. "Marc, I'm sure they are working on it, they still have a couple months left, be patient!" I told him. I knew how he felt. We had been taken advantage of all our lives. I kept telling myself, "We have a signed contract with this agency. They will come through for him. The agent has heard his music and says he can get Marc a record label. Lord, please let Marc get this, he wants it badly!"

If there is one thing I have learned my whole life this is it, "There is no such thing as a coincidence!" There is a divine reason for all things that happen in our lives. There is a reason Marc still has the trach. I don't know what it is but God does. Marc is going to be twenty-three years old soon; we have had the trach almost twenty years. I can still hear David's words ringing in my ears, "He'll not have this trach his whole life." After twenty years I'm still clinging to that. God hasn't taken the trach yet so there is a reason Marc still has it. His life has been a living hell with it but I still tell him, "Use the trach to your advantage Marcus! There is a reason you still have it and God will reveal it to us in due time."

Marc received a contract from a record label a couple of weeks after he called his agent requesting his money back.

The agent informed us that the label had already sent out two contracts that they received back in the mail. They never did reach us. The agent got the label on the phone and they mailed Marc another copy. I can't tell you how Marc felt receiving the contract. Words can't describe it! "I'm going to be rich and famous Mom!" he told me holding the contract in his hand. "Just like I always told you Mom, God is going to give back everything that has been stolen from us over the years."

It reminded me of a scripture I've read a thousand times. The Lord said, "I will return to you the years that the locust has eaten!" (Joel 2:25) The boys and I went without for many years. I spent numerous sleepless nights wondering how I was going pay rent and feed my children. Oftentimes not knowing how I was going to afford Marc's medical supplies. But God was always there; we managed somehow. I had no family to call, no one to depend on. I would pray and tell the Lord what we needed, and it always came in. Sometimes at the very last minute, but he always provided.

The record label contract was requesting a two thousand dollar deposit to help cover cost of production, manufacturing, and distribution. Marcus didn't have that kind of money; neither did Kevin and me. "What am I going to do Mom? It will take me months to save that kind of money." Marc asked. "We are going to ask the Lord to provide it Marc!" I told him seeing the disappointment on his face. I hated that. It was a look I was all too familiar with. I always wanted to make things right for him, but at this time, there isn't anything I can do but pray.

A couple of days after receiving the contract we got a call from the record label. I gave Marc the phone as I listened to him talk to this guy. "Mom, I don't have to pay all of the money at once. He told me to mail him my album, some pictures of myself for my cover and a biography. He said that he can get started on my music and I can make payments." Marc told me as he was hanging up the phone.

The next day we mailed the label everything they needed to start on Marc's album. It's hard for Marc to be patient. He has waited so long for something good to happen in his life. Everyday I hear, "Have we heard from the label yet?" he asks. "Marc, these things take time, it will happen because now we know that this is what God had planned for you all along. God's timing is always perfect, it will happen when we are prepared for it." I told him. "Think about this Marc, were we able to handle this three years ago? No, none of could. God has been positioning us. How much more have you seen the Lord at work in your life? Even in the last year!" I told him. "Yes, I know," Marc said, "I am really blessed Mom." Marcus always seemed to amaze me with his realization of how far the Lord has brought him.

There were still many disappointments in his life. All of us were still dealing with supervised probation. Marc still had several hundreds of dollars to pay for the house arrest. He was trying to get his GED so we took him to the library where he could study and prepare for it. That was frustrating for him; he always did have a difficult time with studies. Kevin and I helped him as much as we could. Sara was starting to give Marc free time at home and the library with out Kevin or I supervising him. I could see a light at the end of the tunnel a lot easier than Marc could. I love Marc more than anything, but I cherished the time I was given without him.

MIRACLES

I've read my story over and over again. It amazes me at how I see the hand of God in the midst of our lives. Oftentimes I wonder about Janet being killed more than twenty years ago. I still ask the Lord, "Why her and not me? My life is a living hell, it always has been!" But I find comfort in knowing that someday he will reveal all things to me.

It's a Friday morning in mid April of 2006. I'm having one of those "Why me Lord?" days. The phone rang and it was Karen from the community works. "Hi Christine, how is everything?" she asked. Karen always had a way of lifting my spirits. "Things are good!" I told her, not wanting to reveal my depressing mood. "I think we may have a job for Marc," she stated excitedly. "One of our other consumers just quit a job at a veterinarian hospital. Marcus may want to talk to the doctor to see if its something he may be interested in." She said. I was so excited I couldn't wait to tell Marc. I got off the phone yelling as I ran through the house trying to locate him. "Marcus! Marcus!" I yelled. Marcus met me in the kitchen. "Karen just called with information on a job for you!" I exclaimed. "Change your clothes and I will take you to apply for the position. Go, quickly, we don't want him to hire someone before you have a chance to talk to him. I'll explain the job to you in the car." Marc didn't ask questions as he ran to him room to change.

"What kind of job is it Mom?" Marc asked as we were getting into the car. "It's at a veterinarian hospital not far from here." I told him. "The doctor is looking for a part time cleaning person. It will be perfect for you!"

Marc was so excited; he had been looking for a job for a long time. With his criminal record against him and the fact that he has a trach, people were not real anxious to hire him. But Doc was different. He hired Marc on the spot. Of course we had to talk to Sara to get her approval since Marc was still on supervised probation. "Do you think Sara will let me take this job Mom?" Marc asked me on our way back home. "I'm sure she will Marc, we will call her when we get home."

Sara was as excited about Marc's job as we were. She set up a time to meet with Doc and Marc was cleared to start the job that Thursday. Kevin dropped Marcus off in the morning on his way to work. When Marc was finished with his cleaning he would call me to pick him up. It was perfect! My mornings were free because I only worked a couple of afternoons a week.

I enjoyed the people I worked with. I loved the customers. Sometimes I felt like I let the Lord down. I would have an opportunity to share him with someone and I didn't. Especially someone who claimed to be a Christian that was very ill. I badly wanted to tell them that Jesus is the healer. This I knew first hand. But I didn't. Most of the time I tried to tell someone that the Lord wanted them healthy, I'd get all kinds of excuses as to why they were sick. I don't understand why a child of God would prefer to be sick than to allow the Lord to heal them. I feel so blessed just in knowing the Lord and what he has for us. Many people would agree that my life has been hard, and it has, but I still have an inner peace that most people have never experienced. I'm not afraid of anything anymore. I can feel the presence of the Lord; I know he is always with me.

I worked with a lady a couple of days a week. Her name was Beth and she was married with five children. I could see my old life in her. Beth was in her thirties, working two jobs trying to make ends meet. From what I understood her husband didn't help out much. I liked Beth, she came across as a strong person, but inside I could tell she was screaming for help. I met her husband one day at the salon. It was nice because she was cutting his hair at the same time Kevin came in for me to cut his. The four of us talked and laughed. "We go camping a lot on the weekends; you two should go with us sometime." Beth said as the guys were leaving. Kevin joked about me going camping because he knew it wasn't one of my favorite things to do. But we agreed that we would go sometime.

One Sunday afternoon I was at work when one of the girls was talking about Beth. I stopped and looked at Ann, one of the other stylists I worked with. I wasn't sure I heard her right. "You knew that Beth's husband passed away a couple days ago, didn't you?" she asked me. I was in shock; I couldn't believe what I was hearing! "No, I didn't! What happened?" I asked. Ann proceeded to tell me, "He died in his sleep. Beth was out of town and his mom is the one that found him."

I felt so bad for Beth! She had five children and no husband. What was even worse is that Kevin and I had an opportunity to share the Lord with him and we didn't. I had such conviction. "I'm going to make a commitment to tell everyone I know about Jesus!" I told Kevin that night while we were sitting out on the deck. He couldn't hardly believe this guy died at the age of thirty-eight. He was so young, we just don't think about death happening to people very often at such a young age.

I decided to call Beth the next morning. "I just heard yesterday about your husband, I'm so sorry." I told her. "How are you doing?" I could tell by her voice she was trying not to cry, "I'm okay, we had the funeral yesterday." I felt so bad for her. "Christine, he didn't have any life insurance, I don't know what I am going to do!" she added. I'm sure everything will be alright." I assured her as we said our goodbyes.

Kevin and I talked about Beth's situation that night over dinner. "I want to help her any way that I can Kevin!" I told him. I've been alone with children to take care of; I know how hard it is! I had no one to help me. We are told by the Lord to take care of widows." I added. I was glad that Kevin agreed with me. I didn't have much money to offer her but I did have Jesus. Beth didn't attend a church, she believed in Jesus so that was a start. I knew that God would use this situation to bring her closer to him. My first responsibility was to pray for her. I started to pray that God would take care of her needs. I couldn't even tell her where to attend church. Kevin and I had left the church we attended for two years. I wasn't happy there. We had been to a few others but just weren't finding our place.

Beth called me a few days later. "I was wondering if you might know of a church that could help me. I have all of these bills due and I can't pay my rent." She said. I could hear hopelessness in her voice. "I do know of a few that you can call." I told her. I gave her a few names and numbers of churches and told her to let me know if she received the help she need. She called me back later that evening. "One of the churches told me they had no funds." She told me. I felt her disappointment as she added, "I had to fill out an application at this other church, and someone will call me back in a couple of days."

I have to admit that anger was rising up in me. "If people can't go to the church, where can they go?" I asked Kevin. "The church should be taking care of people, not sending them away. I'm witnessing to the girl about the goodness of the Lord and the church turns her away." Kevin just looked at me, "You're right!" he said. "I agree that the church has failed the people right here in our own country. We have people dying and going to hell everyday." I was amazed at how much Kevin had grown in the wisdom and knowledge of the Lord. "I understand that there are people that have taken advantage of the church but when a woman has five children and her husband passes away, I believe it is the church's responsibility to give that woman a hand."

My attitude towards the church is now at an all time low. I knew that Beth would make it somehow but she didn't know how to depend on the Lord like I do. I spent years reading and meditating on God's word so I understood his will for my life. Beth's attitude towards the church was even worse than mine at this moment. "Remember the church I told you about that had me fill out the application?" Beth asked me at work a couple weeks later. "Yes, how did that go?" I inquired. "They never did call me back like they said they would so I called them. They only help people that are members of their church." She added. "I'm really sorry Beth." I told her feeling very embarrassed.

I knew I was going to have to take this to the Lord. I wasn't going to not attend church at all because of this. Kevin and I gave thousands of dollars in tithes and offerings each year to the church. It bothered me that we would be denied help if we were in need. This was something I had to roll over to the Lord and not carry myself. I've heard some pastors say, "The World is watching the church!" I think it's sad when we have to turn to the world for help because the church has no funds.

I have talked to children in my own community who have never heard of Jesus. It grieves me. I don't understand what has happened to our churches. I believe it is our responsibility to let everyone we come in contact with know about the Lord. I wouldn't be here today if the pastor that came in to the salon that day and asked me, "Do you know God?" Where would I be if David had not been at the scene of Marc's accident? These men knew their responsibility of being a child of God.

Our father is a God of miracles. He continues to do them in my life everyday. Marcus is a miracle that I'm reminded of every time I look at him. God has brought us through some fire! We have been wounded to the point of no return, or so we thought. But God, who is rich in grace and mercy, heals all our wounds. I truly do believe there is no greater pain than an emotional one. I have had pain buried deep down in the crevices of my being that only the Lord could reach. There is no greater freedom that exists than that which comes from God himself. The greatest miracle of all happens when we ask the Lord to save us. A transformation takes place in our most inner being and we have the full assurance that we belong to him.

"God is Love"! I Corinthians 13 tell us about true love. It is the very nature of God. If you were born again and are away from the Lord, please pray this prayer with me. "My Heavenly Father, I'm coming to you in the name of your precious son Jesus. I've been away from you. I repent of the sin in my life. I want to come home. Please cleanse me from all unrighteousness and create in me a clean heart. I'm giving you my life and pray for your will to be done. Use me Lord Jesus to be a witness for you. Holy Spirit convict me of any sin. Be my teacher and show me things to come. Restore me and make me whole. Thank you Father for your grace and mercy in the name of Jesus! Amen!"

If you prayed that prayer you can know that at this moment you are in right standing with God. He has a plan and purpose for your life.

God does miracles everyday! Its now May of 2006, and my fiftieth birthday is approaching. I went to the mailbox a few days before and received an invitation to a family reunion back home in Pennsylvania. My heart skipped a beat. I was so excited. "I want to talk to you about something," I told Kevin when he came in from work that night. "We got an invitation to my family reunion in July, I want to go!" Kevin was totally surprised, knowing how I felt about my family. "I can take my vacation time and we can go if your sure you want to go." He said. "I do!" I exclaimed. The next day I called Rose to tell her we were coming.

I had not seen most of my family in about thirty years. "Oh Lord, it would be so awesome, please provide the way for us to go." I prayed. I knew the Lord was restoring every area of my life. And my family was at the top of the list. As the day approached for us to go, I started to feel ashamed of my self. I didn't want to go! "What if most of my family wouldn't talk to me? Lord, give me strength to do this!" I prayed. Kevin and I got out of the car and walked toward the city park where the reunion was. My sisters were not there! But a lot of my cousins were. I can't tell you how I felt at that moment. I wanted to laugh and cry at the same time. I saw Janet's sisters and brothers. Her oldest sister raised her baby after she was killed in the car accident. For twenty-eight years I believed that I would someday meet my best friends' baby boy. There he was standing in front of me a grown man! He looked just like Janet. I was so grateful to the Lord at that moment.

I'm not ashamed of my life anymore. I am what I am by the grace of God. I am his workmanship. I'm blessed beyond comprehension. Jesus, my blessed hope, will greet me one day as I enter heaven for the greatest family reunion of all time. I wouldn't miss it for anything in the world. I can honestly say that now I know why my grandmother cried a lot at church and every time someone talked about Jesus. I think about him and I cry also. It is because we love him so much!

I know now that God had a plan for my life. I wasn't a mistake as my brothers and sisters told it. God knew me before I was born. I'm his child. I look back at my miserable life and count it all joy! I'm glad for all that I have been through because it has made me in to the person I am today. Nothing gives me greater pleasure than when someone says to me, "You always have a smile on your face!" I smile because I have become aware of his presence in my life. He's holding me close; protecting me, loving me with his unconditional love. All I want to do with the rest of my life is to share his love with a lost and dying world.

THE END FROM THE BEGINNING

"I'm going to be rich and famous Mom!" I've heard these words a thousand times come out of Marcus' mouth. I've never heard anyone say them with such belief. I've watched him on the stage performing for people. He is such a natural. Like he belongs there. I've often thought that twenty years ago, while Marc was in the coma, that Jesus was talking with him. I believe that God showed Marcus his life. It has been a reality to him since the beginning. I learned long ago that we had an enemy, and that enemy has tried his hardest to keep Marcus from accomplishing the thing that God had predestined him to do.

As I am finishing my story, Marcus has two months left on probation. He has his job that is so very important to him. He works with the community service and his psychologist. "I'm so proud of you Marc." I told him. "You haven't cut on yourself in over a year. Your attitude about life is awesome!" Marc just glared at me and said, "I had to learn to love myself Mom, and I'm not a bad person." I thought for a moment, "Love myself, what a revelation he has!" Marc just taught me something! I needed to love myself also. Up to this point, I've been so disappointed with myself for the decisions I've made in my life. I love me! I'm a great person with a lot to give.

Kevin and I are very happy and content now. I have done what was required of me as a mom. I stood by my son, not denying his wrong doing, but forgiving him for them. Forgiveness is a healer in itself. We all have a bright future ahead of us. I'm a child of the King and I look forward to the rest of my life! I hope you enjoyed my story!

THE END